WRITING SKILLS SUCCESS
IN 20 MINUTES
A DAY

WRITING SKILLS SUCCESS
IN 20 MINUTES A DAY

3rd Edition

LEARNINGEXPRESS®

NEW YORK

Library of Congress Cataloging-in-Publication Data:
    Writing skills success in 20 minutes a day—3rd ed.
        p. cm.
    Includes bibliographical references (p.).
    ISBN 1-57685-495-7 (pbk.)
    1. English language—Grammar—Problems, exercises, etc. 2. English
language—Composition and exercises. I. Title: Writing skills success in twenty minutes a
day. II. Title: Writing skills. III. Title.

PE1112.O45 2005

808'.042—dc22

                                                    2005044127

Printed in the United States of America

9 8 7 6 5 4 3 2

Third Edition

ISBN 1-57685-495-7

For information on LearningExpress, other LearningExpress products, or bulk sales, please write to us at:
    LearningExpress
    55 Broadway
    8th Floor
    New York, NY 10006

Or visit us at:
    www.learnatest.com

Contents

CONTENTS

Introduction ▶

Since you bought this book, you probably want or need to learn more about the process of writing and how to become a better writer. This book will help you acquire the coveted power of the pen in 20 easy steps. It covers the basics of writing: punctuation, usage, diction, and organization. You'll find no fluff in this book; it's for busy people who want to learn as much as they can as efficiently as possible. Each lesson contains enough illustrations for you to get the idea, opportunities to practice the skills, and suggestions for using them in your daily life.

Many people fear a blank sheet of paper or an empty computer screen. "I just don't know what to write. Even when I know what I want to say, I'm afraid it will come out looking wrong or sounding stupid."

But that's one of the things to love about writing. Writing is a process. The first time you write a draft, it doesn't matter if your writing comes out wrong or sounds stupid to you because you can change it as often as you want. You can go over it until you're completely satisfied or until you need to shift gears. You can show your draft to your friends or family and get a response before you ever make it public.

Don't put pressure on yourself by thinking you're going to write a perfect first draft. No one can sit down and write polished memos, reports, or letters without changing (or revising) them at least slightly. Even professionals have to revise their work. For instance, writer Ernest Hemingway had to revise the last page of his famous novel *A Farewell to Arms* 39 times before he was satisfied. You probably won't want to revise anything that many times before the final copy, but even if you write two or three drafts, you certainly aren't alone in your need for revision.

Writing has three distinct advantages over speaking:

1. In writing, you can take it back. The spoken word, however, cannot be revised. Once you make a statement verbally, it affects your listeners in a particular way and you can't "take it back" or rephrase it to the point that the first statement is forgotten. However, if you write a statement and, after looking at it, realize that it sounds offensive or incorrect, you can revise it before giving it to the intended audience. Writing is a careful, thoughtful way of communicating.

2. Writing forces you to clarify your thoughts. If you're having trouble writing, it's often because you're not yet finished with the thinking part. Sometimes, just sitting down and writing whatever is on your mind helps you discover and organize what you think.

3. Another advantage is permanence. Ideas presented in writing carry far more weight than spoken ideas. Additionally, they can be reviewed and referred to in their exact, original form. Spoken ideas rely upon the sometimes inaccurate memories of other people.

Writing is nothing more than thought on paper—considered, organized thought. Many people are protective of their thoughts and, therefore, prefer to keep them hidden inside their heads. Many great ideas and observations are never born because their creators won't express them. This book can help you express your ideas in clear, grammatically correct ways. After you learn how to insert commas and semicolons correctly, use verbs to create strong images in your writing, and the other basic skills taught in this book, you'll gain confidence in your writing ability. In fact, you'll be able to move forward and master more complex writing concerns after you get the basics down. More and more jobs these days require at least some writing, so the skills you learn in this book will be put to good use.

The lessons in this book are designed to be completed in about 20 minutes each. If you do a lesson every weekday, you can finish the whole course in about a month. However, you may find another approach that works better for you. You'll find you make more progress, though, if you complete at least two lessons a week. If you leave too much time between lessons, you'll forget what you've learned. You may want to start with the pretest that begins on page 1. It will show you what you already know and what you need to learn about grammar, mechanics, and punctuation. Then, when you've finished the book, you can take a posttest to see how much you've improved.

If you practice what you've learned in this book, it won't take long for other people to notice the new and improved you. So dive into the first lesson and get ready to improve your writing skills. Good luck!

Pretest

efore you start your study of grammar and writing skills, you may want to get an idea of how much you already know and how much you need to learn. If that's the case, take the pretest that follows.

The pretest consists of 50 multiple-choice questions covering all the lessons in this book. Naturally, 50 questions can't cover every single concept or rule you will learn by working through these pages. So even if you answer all of the questions on the pretest correctly, it's almost guaranteed that you will find a few ideas or rules in this book that you didn't already know. On the other hand, if you get a lot of the answers wrong on this pretest, don't despair. This book will show you how to improve your grammar and writing, step by step.

So use this pretest for a general idea of how much of what's in this book you already know. If you get a high score, you may be able to spend less time with this book than you originally planned. If you get a low score, you may find that you will need more than 20 minutes a day to get through each chapter and learn all the grammar and mechanics concepts you need.

There's an answer sheet you can use for filling in the correct answers on page 3. Or, if you prefer, simply circle the answer numbers in this book. If the book doesn't belong to you, write the numbers 1–50 on a piece of paper and record your answers there. Take as much time as you need to complete this short test. When you finish, check your answers against the answer key that follows. Each answer tells you which lesson of this book teaches you about the grammatical rule in that question.

1.	ⓐ	ⓑ	ⓒ	ⓓ
2.	ⓐ	ⓑ	ⓒ	ⓓ
3.	ⓐ	ⓑ	ⓒ	ⓓ
4.	ⓐ	ⓑ	ⓒ	ⓓ
5.	ⓐ	ⓑ	ⓒ	ⓓ
6.	ⓐ	ⓑ	ⓒ	ⓓ
7.	ⓐ	ⓑ	ⓒ	ⓓ
8.	ⓐ	ⓑ	ⓒ	ⓓ
9.	ⓐ	ⓑ	ⓒ	ⓓ
10.	ⓐ	ⓑ	ⓒ	ⓓ
11.	ⓐ	ⓑ	ⓒ	ⓓ
12.	ⓐ	ⓑ	ⓒ	ⓓ
13.	ⓐ	ⓑ	ⓒ	ⓓ
14.	ⓐ	ⓑ	ⓒ	ⓓ
15.	ⓐ	ⓑ	ⓒ	ⓓ
16.	ⓐ	ⓑ	ⓒ	ⓓ
17.	ⓐ	ⓑ	ⓒ	ⓓ

18.	ⓐ	ⓑ	ⓒ	ⓓ
19.	ⓐ	ⓑ	ⓒ	ⓓ
20.	ⓐ	ⓑ	ⓒ	ⓓ
21.	ⓐ	ⓑ	ⓒ	ⓓ
22.	ⓐ	ⓑ	ⓒ	ⓓ
23.	ⓐ	ⓑ	ⓒ	ⓓ
24.	ⓐ	ⓑ	ⓒ	ⓓ
25.	ⓐ	ⓑ	ⓒ	ⓓ
26.	ⓐ	ⓑ	ⓒ	ⓓ
27.	ⓐ	ⓑ	ⓒ	ⓓ
28.	ⓐ	ⓑ	ⓒ	ⓓ
29.	ⓐ	ⓑ	ⓒ	ⓓ
30.	ⓐ	ⓑ	ⓒ	ⓓ
31.	ⓐ	ⓑ	ⓒ	ⓓ
32.	ⓐ	ⓑ	ⓒ	ⓓ
33.	ⓐ	ⓑ	ⓒ	ⓓ
34.	ⓐ	ⓑ	ⓒ	ⓓ

35.	ⓐ	ⓑ	ⓒ	ⓓ
36.	ⓐ	ⓑ	ⓒ	ⓓ
37.	ⓐ	ⓑ	ⓒ	ⓓ
38.	ⓐ	ⓑ	ⓒ	ⓓ
39.	ⓐ	ⓑ	ⓒ	ⓓ
40.	ⓐ	ⓑ	ⓒ	ⓓ
41.	ⓐ	ⓑ	ⓒ	ⓓ
42.	ⓐ	ⓑ	ⓒ	ⓓ
43.	ⓐ	ⓑ	ⓒ	ⓓ
44.	ⓐ	ⓑ	ⓒ	ⓓ
45.	ⓐ	ⓑ	ⓒ	ⓓ
46.	ⓐ	ⓑ	ⓒ	ⓓ
47.	ⓐ	ⓑ	ⓒ	ⓓ
48.	ⓐ	ⓑ	ⓒ	ⓓ
49.	ⓐ	ⓑ	ⓒ	ⓓ
50.	ⓐ	ⓑ	ⓒ	ⓓ

▶ Pretest

1. Which version of the sentence is correctly capitalized?

    a. Last Tuesday, my Mother, my Aunt Nancy, and I went to the museum to see an exhibit of Egyptian sculpture.

    b. Last Tuesday, my mother, my Aunt Nancy, and I went to the museum to see an exhibit of Egyptian sculpture.

    c. Last Tuesday, my mother, my aunt Nancy, and I went to the Museum to see an exhibit of Egyptian sculpture.

    d. Last Tuesday, my mother, my aunt Nancy, and I went to the museum to see an exhibit of Egyptian Sculpture.

2. Which of the underlined words in the following sentence should be capitalized?

    The <u>governor</u> gave a speech at the <u>fourth</u> of July picnic, which was held at my <u>cousin's</u> farm five miles <u>east</u> of town.

    a. governor
    b. fourth
    c. cousin's
    d. east

3. Which of the underlined words in the following sentence should be capitalized?

    "Last <u>semester</u>, I wrote my <u>history</u> report on the Korean <u>war</u>," my <u>sister</u> told me.

    a. semester
    b. history
    c. war
    d. sister

4. Which version uses periods correctly?

    a. Dr Harrison will speak at a hotel in Chicago, Ill, on Thurs at 3:00 P.M.

    b. Dr. Harrison will speak at a hotel in Chicago, Ill, on Thurs at 3:00 PM.

    c. Dr Harrison will speak at a hotel in Chicago, Ill, on Thurs. at 3:00 P.M.

    d. Dr. Harrison will speak at a hotel in Chicago, Ill., on Thurs. at 3:00 P.M.

5. Which version uses punctuation correctly?

    a. Be careful. The stairs are slippery?

    b. Be careful! The stairs are slippery.

    c. Be careful? The stairs are slippery!

    d. Be careful, the stairs are slippery?

6. Which of the following is a sentence fragment, that is, NOT a complete sentence?

    a. Hearing the thunder, the lifeguard ordered us out of the water.

    b. Turn off the lights.

    c. Sunday afternoon spent reading and playing computer games.

    d. I was surprised to see that my neighbor had written a letter to the editor.

7. Three of the following sentences are either run-ons or comma splices. Which one is NOT a faulty sentence?

    a. The newspapers are supposed to be delivered by 7:00, but I am usually finished before 6:45.

    b. I called the delivery service this morning, they told me the shipment would arrive on time.

    c. Look in the closet you should find it there.

    d. I was the first to sign the petition Harry was second.

8. Which version is punctuated correctly?
   a. Charlotte, who ran in the Boston Marathon last year will compete in this year's New York Marathon.
   b. Charlotte who ran in the Boston Marathon, last year, will compete in this year's New York Marathon.
   c. Charlotte who ran in the Boston Marathon last year, will compete in this year's New York Marathon.
   d. Charlotte, who ran in the Boston Marathon last year, will compete in this year's New York Marathon.

9. Which version is punctuated correctly?
   a. The park service will not allow anyone, who does not have a camping permit, to use this campground.
   b. The park service will not allow anyone who does not have a camping permit to use this campground.
   c. The park service will not allow anyone, who does not have a camping permit to use this campground.
   d. The park service will not allow anyone who does not have a camping permit, to use this campground.

10. Which version is punctuated correctly?
   a. As soon as she finished her dinner, Lisa, who is a volunteer at the hospital, reported for her shift.
   b. As soon as she finished her dinner Lisa, who is a volunteer at the hospital reported for her shift.
   c. As soon as she finished, her dinner, Lisa who is a volunteer at the hospital, reported for her shift.
   d. As soon as she finished her dinner, Lisa who is a volunteer at the hospital reported for her shift.

11. Which of the underlined portions of the sentence below is punctuated incorrectly?

   My mother was born on (**a**) <u>December 15, 1944,</u> in Kingwood, West (**b**) <u>Virginia, when</u> she was (**c**) <u>five, her</u> family moved to (**d**) <u>347 Benton Street, Zanesville, Ohio</u>.

   a. December 15, 1944,
   b. Virginia, when
   c. five, her
   d. 347 Benton Street, Zanesville, Ohio.

12. Which version is punctuated correctly?
   a. Yes I would like to receive the credit card application and please send it as soon as you can to my home address.
   b. Yes, I would like to receive the credit card application and please send it, as soon as you can to my home address.
   c. Yes, I would like to receive the credit card application and, please send it as soon as you can to my home address.
   d. Yes, I would like to receive the credit card application, and please send it as soon as you can to my home address.

13. Which version is punctuated correctly?
   a. I'm sorry, Bart, that you cannot meet us for dinner tonight. We'll phone you again next Friday.
   b. I'm sorry, Bart that you cannot meet us for dinner tonight. We'll phone you again next Friday.
   c. I'm sorry Bart that you cannot meet us for dinner tonight. We'll phone you again next Friday.
   d. I'm sorry, Bart, that you cannot meet us for dinner tonight, we'll phone you again next Friday.

14. Which is the correct punctuation for the under-lined portion?

The weather forecasters are predicting ten inches of snow <u>tonight therefore</u> the annual chili supper will be rescheduled for next week.

   a. tonight, therefore
   b. tonight, therefore,
   c. tonight; therefore,
   d. tonight, therefore;

15. Which is the correct punctuation for the under-lined portion?

You may choose to read any two of the follow-ing <u>novels The</u> Great Gatsby, Song of Solomon, Sophie's Choice, The Color Purple, The Bell Jar, and The Invisible Man.

   a. novels, *The*
   b. novels: *The*
   c. novels; *the*
   d. novels. *The*

16. Which version is punctuated correctly?
   a. One of my complaints—if you really want to know is that the recycling bins are not clearly labeled.
   b. One of my complaints—if you really want to know—is that the recycling bins are not clearly labeled.
   c. One of my complaints, if you really want to know—is that the recycling bins are not clearly labeled.
   d. One of my complaints if you really want to know is that the recycling bins are not clearly labeled.

17. Which version is punctuated correctly?
   a. You will find boys' shirts in the childrens' department.
   b. You will find boy's shirts in the children's department.
   c. You will find boys' shirts in the children's department.
   d. You will find boy's shirts in the childrens' department.

18. Which version is punctuated correctly?
   a. Whose coat is this? Is it yours or Eric's?
   b. Whose coat is this? Is it your's or Eric's?
   c. Who's coat is this? Is it your's or Eric's?
   d. Who's coat is this? Is it yours or Eric's?

19. Which version is punctuated correctly?
   a. "May I ride with you?" asked Del. "I can't get my car started."
   b. May I ride with you? asked Del. "I can't get my car started."
   c. "May I ride with you? asked Del. I can't get my car started."
   d. "May I ride with you"? asked Del, "I can't get my car started."

20. Which of the following should be placed in quo-tation marks and should NOT be italicized or underlined?
   a. the name of a ship
   b. the title of a poem
   c. the title of a novel
   d. the name of a newspaper

21. Which version uses hyphens correctly?
   a. The well-known singer-songwriter gave a three hour concert.
   b. The well known singer songwriter gave a three-hour concert.
   c. The well-known singer-songwriter gave a three-hour concert.
   d. The well known singer-songwriter gave a three hour concert.

22. Which of the following should NOT be hyphenated?
   a. twenty-one students
   b. two-inch nails
   c. a thirty-minute interview
   d. ten-feet of rope

23. Which version uses parentheses correctly?
   a. I plan to do my geography report on the Central American country of Belize (formerly known as British Honduras).
   b. I plan to do my geography report on the (Central American country of) Belize, formerly known as British Honduras.
   c. I plan to do my (geography) report on the Central American country of Belize, formerly known as British Honduras.
   d. I plan to do my geography report on the Central American country (of Belize) formerly known as British Honduras.

For questions 24 and 25, choose the correct verb form.

24. Last night, Rita _____ a standing ovation for her performance.
   a. has gotten
   b. gotten
   c. will get
   d. got

25. Brandon _____ his camera so he could photograph the basketball game.
   a. brang
   b. brought
   c. bring
   d. had brung

26. Which of the following underlined verbs is NOT written in the correct tense?

Last year, I (**a**) <u>vacationed</u> in Jamaica. I (**b**) <u>sunbathe</u> on the beach every morning. In the afternoons, I (**c**) <u>explored</u> the island, and when evening came, I (**d**) <u>couldn't wait</u> to change my clothes and try another local restaurant.

   a. vacationed
   b. sunbathe
   c. explored
   d. couldn't wait

27. Choose the version that correctly rewrites the following sentence in the active voice.

I was taken to the public library by my sister before I was able to read.

   a. Before I was able to read, I was taken to the public library by my sister.
   b. Before learning to read, my sister took me to the public library.
   c. Before I was able to read, my sister took me to the public library.
   d. I was taken to the public library before I knew how to read, by my sister.

28. Which of the following sentences is in the passive voice?
   a. On Saturday nights, we made popcorn.
   b. Our bowls were filled and brought into the living room.
   c. We sat on the floor and watched the movie we had rented.
   d. One of us usually fell asleep before the movie was over.

For questions 29 and 30, choose the verb that agrees with the subject of the sentence.

29. Neither of the boys _____ to basketball camp.
   a. have been
   b. were
   c. is been
   d. has been

30. The music teacher, along with several of her students, _____ to attend the concert on Sunday evening.
   a. is planning
   b. are planning
   c. plan
   d. have planned

31. Choose the subject that agrees with the verb in the following sentence.

_____ of the customers have complained about poor service.

   a. One
   b. Neither
   c. Each
   d. Some

32. In which of the following sentences is the underlined verb NOT in agreement with the subject of the sentence?
   a. Where <u>are</u> the forms you want me to fill out?
   b. Which <u>is</u> the correct form?
   c. Here <u>is</u> the forms you need to complete.
   d. There <u>are</u> two people who still need to complete the form.

33. In which of the following sentences is the underlined pronoun incorrect?
   a. Alicia and <u>me</u> want to spend Saturday at Six Flags Amusement Park.
   b. Either Sam or William will bring <u>his</u> CD player to the party.
   c. She and <u>I</u> will work together on the project.
   d. Why won't you let <u>her</u> come with us?

34. In which of the following sentences is the underlined pronoun incorrect?
   a. Francine can run much faster than <u>me.</u>
   b. Erin and Bob are painting the house <u>themselves.</u>
   c. Five members of the team and <u>I</u> will represent our school.
   d. Our neighbors gave <u>us</u> some tomatoes from their garden.

For questions 35–38, choose the option that correctly completes the sentence.

35. Four band members and _____ were chosen to attend the state competition. One of _____ will do the driving.
   a. me, we
   b. me, us
   c. I, we
   d. I, us

36. Marcus _____ the bags of groceries on the kitchen table fifteen minutes ago.
   a. had sat
   b. set
   c. sit
   d. sat

37. About five minutes after the sun _____,
my alarm goes off, and _____ time to
get up.
  a. raises, it's
  b. raises, its
  c. rises, it's
  d. rises, its

38. Paula did _____ on the test, but Georgia
had the _____ score in the class.
  a. good, better
  b. good, best
  c. well, better
  d. well, best

39. Which of the sentences is clearly and correctly
written?
  a. Driving along the country road, a deer ran in
    front of us.
  b. A deer ran in front of us while driving along
    the country road.
  c. As we were driving along the country road, a
    deer ran in front of us.
  d. Running in front of us, we saw the deer, driv-
    ing along the country road.

For questions 40–46, choose the option that correctly
completes the sentence.

40. If we divide this pizza _____ the five
people here, there won't be _____ pieces
left over.
  a. among, any
  b. among, no
  c. between, any
  d. between, no

41. Yesterday, I _____ the campers to the
_____ we had chosen near the river.
  a. lead, cite
  b. lead, site
  c. led, cite
  d. led, site

42. As we have done in the _____, we will
_____ at the coffeehouse at 10:00 A.M.
  a. past, meet
  b. past, meat
  c. passed, meet
  d. passed, meat

43. As you can _____ see, there has been a
_____ in the water pipe.
  a. planely, brake
  b. planely, break
  c. plainly, brake
  d. plainly, break

44. Do you know _____ Teresa will
_____ to join our organization?
  a. weather, choose
  b. weather, chose
  c. whether, choose
  d. whether, chose

45. _____ are the magazines that
_____ to be stacked on this table?
  a. Wear, used
  b. Wear, use
  c. Where, used
  d. Where, use

46. Do you _____ if Serena Williams
_____ the tournament?
  a. know, one
  b. know, won
  c. no, one
  d. no, won

47. Which of the following phrases contains a redundancy? (It repeats words that express the same idea.)
   a. I did not go to the shopping mall.
   b. She always does very well in school.
   c. The judges have temporarily delayed the competition until later.
   d. Liz and Lauren have both contributed greatly to the fundraising campaign.

48. Which of the following sentences contains a cliché?
   a. The room was so quiet, you could hear a pin drop.
   b. Your plan is not in accordance with the regulations set down by the review board.
   c. The stars were pinpricks in the tarpaper sky.
   d. Due to the fact that it snowed, the trip was canceled.

49. Which version has a consistent point of view?
   a. The history of English is divided into three periods. You could mark the earliest one at about the fifth century A.D.
   b. You can say that the history of English could be divided into three periods, and I know the earliest one begins about the fifth century A.D.
   c. The history of English is divided into three periods. The earliest one begins at about the fifth century A.D.
   d. I learned that the history of English is divided into three periods and that you begin the earliest one at about the fifth century A.D.

50. Which version has a parallel structure?
   a. We write for a variety of purposes: in expressing our feelings, to convey information, to persuade, or to give pleasure.
   b. We write for a variety of purposes: to express our feelings, convey information, persuasion, or giving pleasure.
   c. We write for a variety of purposes: an expression of our feelings, conveying information, persuade, or to give pleasure.
   d. We write for a variety of purposes: to express our feelings, to convey information, to persuade, or to give pleasure.

▶ Answer Key

If you miss any of the answers, you can find help for that kind of question in the lesson shown to the right of the answer.

1. b. Lesson 1	**26. b.** Lesson 10
2. b. Lesson 1	**27. c.** Lesson 11
3. c. Lesson 1	**28. b.** Lesson 11
4. d. Lesson 2	**29. d.** Lesson 12
5. b. Lesson 2	**30. a.** Lesson 12
6. c. Lesson 3	**31. d.** Lesson 12
7. a. Lesson 3	**32. c.** Lesson 12
8. d. Lesson 4	**33. a.** Lesson 13
9. b. Lesson 4	**34. a.** Lesson 13
10. a. Lesson 4	**35. d.** Lesson 13
11. b. Lessons 5, 6	**36. b.** Lesson 14
12. d. Lesson 5	**37. c.** Lesson 14
13. a. Lesson 5	**38. d.** Lesson 14
14. c. Lesson 6	**39. c.** Lesson 15
15. b. Lesson 6	**40. a.** Lesson 15
16. b. Lesson 7	**41. d.** Lesson 16
17. c. Lesson 7	**42. a.** Lesson 16
18. a. Lesson 7	**43. d.** Lesson 16
19. a. Lesson 8	**44. c.** Lesson 17
20. b. Lesson 8	**45. c.** Lesson 17
21. c. Lesson 9	**46. b.** Lesson 17
22. d. Lesson 9	**47. c.** Lesson 18
23. a. Lesson 9	**48. a.** Lesson 18
24. d. Lesson 10	**49. c.** Lesson 19
25. b. Lesson 10	**50. d.** Lesson 19

1 ▶ Capitalization

LESSON SUMMARY

Today, you'll learn about the fine points of capitalization. This chapter divides capitalization rules into two kinds: general rules governing capitalization and specific rules regarding proper nouns and adjectives.

tart by seeing just how much you already know about the proper use of capital letters. On the next page, you see the same passage written twice. The first column, called **Problem**, contains no capitalization at all—definitely a problem in writing! Circle those letters you think should be capitalized in the **Problem** column, and then check yourself against the **Solution** column.

Problem

when I first saw the black hills on january 2, 1995, i was shocked by their beauty. we had just spent new year's day in sioux falls, south dakota, and had headed west toward our home in denver, colorado. as we traveled along interstate 90, i could see the black hills rising slightly in the distance. after driving through the badlands and stopping at wall drug in wall, south dakota, the evergreen-covered hills broke the barren monotony of the landscape. my oldest daughter said, "dad, look! there's something that's not all white." we saw mount rushmore and custer state park, the home of the largest herd of buffalo in north america. we also drove the treacherous spearfish canyon road. fortunately, our jeep cherokee had no trouble with the ice and snow on the winding road. we were unable to see needles national park because the needles highway was snowed shut. winter may not be the best time to see these sights, but we enjoyed them nonetheless.

Solution

When I first saw the Black Hills on January 2, 1995, I was shocked by their beauty. We had just spent New Year's Day in Sioux Falls, South Dakota, and had headed west toward our home in Denver, Colorado. As we traveled along Interstate 90, I could see the Black Hills rising slightly in the distance. After driving through the Badlands and stopping at Wall Drug in Wall, South Dakota, the evergreen-covered hills broke the barren monotony of the landscape. My oldest daughter said, "Dad, look! There's something that's not all white." We saw Mount Rushmore and Custer State Park, the home of the largest herd of buffalo in North America. We also drove the treacherous Spearfish Canyon Road. Fortunately, our Jeep Cherokee had no trouble with the ice and snow on the winding road. We were unable to see Needles National Park because the Needles Highway was snowed shut. Winter may not be the best time to see these sights, but we enjoyed them nonetheless.

How did you do? As you progress through the lesson, try to identify the specific rules that you missed.

▶ General Capitalization Rules

This table summarizes general capitalization rules. Rules relating to specific categories of proper nouns are addressed in the next section.

CAPITALIZATION RULES

RULE	EXAMPLE
Capitalize the first word of a sentence. If the first word is a number, write it as a word.	This is the first word of the sentence. Three of us worked the early shift.
Capitalize the pronoun *I* or the contraction *I'm*, and the abbreviations *B.C.* or *A.D.*	The group left when **I** asked them to go. The manuscript was dated 501 **A.D.**
Capitalize the first word of a quotation. Do not capitalize the first word of a partial quotation.	I said, "What's the name of your dog?" He called me "the worst excuse for a student" he had ever seen.

Here is an example of a dialogue that illustrates these rules. (A note about paragraphing in dialogue: Each time a speaker finishes, begin a new paragraph.)

"**G**ood afternoon," said the personal trainer as **I** walked into the gym.

"**G**ood afternoon!" **I** replied, excited to get started.

"**Y**ou must be Ms. Milner. **I**'m Jennifer Burnett. **I**t's very nice to meet you."

"**T**ell me about your current workout routine, Jennifer. **I**'m eager to put together a brand-new exercise program for you."

I smiled and said, "**I**t's so nice to be working with you. **I** heard you were a '**t**rue fitness guru.'"

Practice

Check your ability to apply these rules in the following practice questions. Choose the correctly capitalized option from each of the sets below. Answers to each set of questions can be found at the end of the lesson.

1. a. the movie terrified me at first. after a few minutes, i began to calm down.
   b. The movie terrified me at first. after a few minutes, I began to calm down.
   c. The movie terrified me at first. After a few minutes, I began to calm down.

2. a. "what are you doing?" my supervisor asked. "trying to finish the memo I've been writing," i replied.
   b. "What are you doing?" my supervisor asked. "Trying to finish the memo I've been writing," I replied.
   c. "What are you doing?" My supervisor asked. "Trying to finish the memo I've been writing," I replied.

3. **a.** we saw pottery made in 1550 A.D.
   b. We saw pottery made in 1550 a.d.
   c. We saw pottery made in 1550 A.D.

4. **a.** After the game is over, I want to watch the interviews with the players.
   b. after the game is over, I want to watch the interviews with the players.
   c. After the game is over, i want to watch the interviews with the players.

▶ Proper Nouns and Proper Adjectives

All proper nouns and proper adjectives—ones that name a specific person, place, or thing—must be capitalized, but remembering which nouns and adjectives are proper can be difficult. The tables that follow lay out the most common categories of proper nouns and adjectives. Each section begins with a table that illustrates 5–7 related rules, followed by several practice exercises.

PROPER NOUNS, PART ONE	
CATEGORY OF PROPER NOUNS	EXAMPLES
days of the week	Friday, Saturday
months	January, February
holidays	Christmas, Halloween
historical events, periods, documents	Civil War (historical event), Dark Ages (historical period), Declaration of Independence (document)
special events, calendar events	Pebble Beach Fall Classic, Renaissance Festival, Green River Days (special events); Labor Day, Father's Day (calendar events)
names of people and places	John Doe, Lincoln Center, Sears Tower

Practice
Using these rules, choose the correctly capitalized version of each of the following pairs.

5. **a.** Chaucer was one of the foremost poets from the Middle ages.
   b. Chaucer was one of the foremost poets from the Middle Ages.

6. **a.** The Martins will begin their summer with a weeklong Memorial Day celebration at a beautiful lakeside hotel.
   b. The Martins will begin their summer with a weeklong Memorial day celebration at a beautiful Lakeside hotel.

7. **a.** We studied the declaration of independence in History class.
   b. We studied the Declaration of Independence in history class.

8. **a.** Judy has two Uncles who fought in world war II.
   b. Judy has two uncles who fought in World War II.

PROPER NOUNS, PART TWO	
CATEGORY OF PROPER NOUNS	EXAMPLES
names of structures and buildings	Washington Memorial, Empire State Building
names of trains, ships, aircraft, and other modes of transportation	Queen Elizabeth, Discovery, Sioux Lines, TransWorld Airlines
names of products	Corn King hams, Dodge Intrepid
names of officials	Mayor Daley, President Clinton
works of art and literature	*Black Elk Speaks* (book), "Mending Wall" (poem), Mona Lisa (painting)
ethnic groups, races, languages, nationalities	Asian American, Caucasian, French, Indian

Practice

Choose the correctly capitalized version of each of the following pairs.

9. a. My book group selected *the known world* by Edward P. Jones.
   b. My book group selected *The Known World* by Edward P. Jones.

10. a. We caught a Vanguard Airlines flight to Orlando.
   b. We caught a Vanguard airlines flight to Orlando.

11. a. The Talmud is a guide to the teachings of judaism.
   b. The Talmud is a guide to the teachings of Judaism.

12. a. Paul has an editing job with Meredith Publishing.
   b. Paul has an Editing job with Meredith Publishing.

13. a. The University of Michigan has an excellent Business School.
   b. The university of Michigan has an excellent business school.

14. a. Dr. Gallagher researched her book at the Library of Congress.
   b. Dr. Gallagher researched her book at the Library of congress.

PROPER NOUNS, PART THREE	
CATEGORY OF PROPER NOUNS	**EXAMPLES**
cities, states, and governmental units	Des Moines, Iowa; Barrow, Alaska; Republic of South Africa
streets, highways, and roads	Grand Avenue, Interstate 29, Deadwood Road
landmarks and geographical locations	Continental Divide, Grand Canyon
public areas and bodies of water	Superior Forest, Missouri River
institutions, organizations, and businesses	Dartmouth College, Lions Club, Dodge Trucks

Practice

Choose the correctly capitalized version of each of the following pairs.

15. a. Both English and French are spoken in Montreal.
b. Both english and french are spoken in Montreal.

16. a. Near a body of water called firth and forth, you can see Edinburgh, Scotland.
b. Near a body of water called Firth and Forth, you can see Edinburgh, Scotland.

17. a. There is an incredible view of the Pacific ocean from Big Sur, California.
b. There is an incredible view of the Pacific Ocean from Big Sur, California.

18. a. Mount Everest, which is in the middle of the Himalayan Range, is the highest mountain in the world.
b. Mount Everest, which is in the middle of the Himalayan Range, is the highest mountain in the World.

19. a. I have traveled on the Garden state Parkway, a main highway in New Jersey.
b. I have traveled on the Garden State Parkway, a main highway in New Jersey.

Proper Adjectives

Proper adjectives are adjectives—that is, words that modify nouns—formed from a proper noun, often the name of a place. For instance, the proper noun *Canada* becomes the proper adjective *Canadian* when it modifies another noun, as in *Canadian bacon*. Note that the noun is not capitalized unless it is a proper noun in its own right.

Examples:
English **m**uffin, **P**olish **s**ausage, **J**apanese **y**en

Practice

Choose the correctly capitalized version of each of the following pairs.

20. a. Some residents of ireland still speak the Gaelic Language.
b. Some residents of Ireland still speak the Gaelic language.

21. a. Frida Kahlo, a Mexican artist, painted many self-portraits.
b. Frida Kahlo, a mexican artist, painted many self-portraits.

22. a. The actress in the play tried to speak with a Scottish accent.
b. The Actress in the play tried to speak with a Scottish accent.

23. a. I will never attempt to swim the English channel.
b. I will never attempt to swim the English Channel.

24. a. The new Ethiopian Restaurant was getting rave reviews.
b. The new Ethiopian restaurant was getting rave reviews.

▶ When NOT to Capitalize

Putting in capital letters where they don't belong is as bad as leaving them out where they do belong. Watch for these capitalization traps.

- Avoid unnecessarily capitalizing compass directions; however, direction words that refer to a specific area of the country should be capitalized.
  Examples:
  We headed **w**est after the Depression.
  The future of the country was cultivated in the **W**est.
- Avoid unnecessarily capitalizing the words referring to family members. Capitalize them only when they are used as names. If a possessive pronoun (*my, our, your, his, her, their*) comes before the word referring to a family member, the family word is not capitalized.
  Examples:
  When **U**ncle Harry visited last winter, none of my other **u**ncles came to see him.
  After my **m**other called me for lunch, **F**ather served the entree.
- Avoid unnecessarily capitalizing the seasons of the year or parts of the academic year.
  Example:
  If the university offers History of Education 405 in the **s**pring **s**emester, Horace can graduate in May.

- Avoid unnecessarily capitalizing school subjects. They should be capitalized only if they are part of the name of a specific course.
  Examples:
  I try to avoid **m**ath courses because I'm not very good at them.
  Betsy is taking **A**lgebra II and **T**rigonometry I next semester.
- Avoid unnecessarily capitalizing words modified by proper adjectives.
  Examples:
  Polish **s**ausage, not Polish Sausage
  Mexican **r**estaurant, not Mexican Restaurant

Practice
Choose the correctly capitalized version of each of the following pairs.

25. a. Digging the Canal through Panama took many years.
b. Digging the canal through Panama took many years.

26. a. The Smoky Mountains are in the Southeastern part of the country.
b. The Smoky Mountains are in the southeastern part of the country.

27. a. Nicholi Milani does more business in the East than in the West.
b. Nicholi Milani does more business in the east than in the west.

28. a. The Southeast was affected by many bad storms last year.
b. The southeast was affected by many bad storms last year.

29. a. Marianne had never been as far East as Columbus, Ohio.
b. Marianne had never been as far east as Columbus, Ohio.

► Answers

1. c.		**16.** b.	
2. b.		**17.** b.	
3. c.		**18.** a.	
4. a.		**19.** b.	
5. b.		**20.** b.	
6. a.		**21.** a.	
7. b.		**22.** a.	
8. b.		**23.** b.	
9. b.		**24.** b.	
10. a.		**25.** b.	
11. b.		**26.** b.	
12. a.		**27.** a.	
13. b.		**28.** a.	
14. a.		**29.** b.	
15. a.			

Skill Building until Next Time

Find the obituaries in your local newspaper. Examine the capitalization used in the writing. How many of the rules you learned today can you find represented in a single obituary notice?

2 ▶ Periods, Question Marks, and Exclamation Points

LESSON SUMMARY

This lesson shows you which punctuation marks to use to end sentences. These are sometimes referred to as "endmarks." It also shows you other ways in which periods are used.

The exercise that follows reviews Lesson 1, Capitalization, and gives you an opportunity to see what you already know about periods and endmarks. Correct the capitalization in the **Problem** column on the next page, adding periods, question marks, and exclamation points where you think they should go. Check yourself with the **Solution** column as you go.

Problem

William Reese had not been inside Oak Hill high school for five years when he graduated, William left harrisburg, Pennsylvania to attend the university of Wisconsin He was looking forward to seeing his old Teachers, and he was sure they would be surprised about how successful he had become

william was not a model high school student In fact, he was awful his guidance counselor, Ms Lewis, always told him that she couldn't understand how someone as bright as he was could get such poor grades William came very close to failing at least three of his subjects every marking period he especially disliked math and science

After school on Wednesdays, Thursdays, and fridays, William would get into his old Honda civic and drive to Cedar street, where he worked the afternoon shift at Milton's bookstore This was his favorite place to be he loved being surrounded by books, and when he wasn't helping customers, he would sit behind the counter and read as much as he could During these afternoon shifts, William read some books that changed his life one of his favorites was *on the Road* by Jack Kerouac his reading inspired him to keep a Journal, which he wrote in every day

When it was time to consider college william spent many hours with Ms Lewis thinking about his future After reading his journals, Ms Lewis suggested that perhaps William would be happiest at a College where he could study creative writing The rest is history

William was one of the Top Students in the creative writing Program at the University of Wisconsin during his Junior Year, one of his essays was accepted for publication in a National magazine, and soon after that, William received a call from an editor at Bound brook publishing who wanted to publish a collection of William's short stories as soon as the book was published William sent a copy to Ms Lewis thanking her for her support and advice

Now he was on his way back to visit Ms Lewis and his other teachers, who were probably all asking the same question Can this be the same William Reese

Solution

William Reese had not been inside Oak Hill High School for five years. When he graduated, William left Harrisburg, Pennsylvania to attend the University of Wisconsin. He was looking forward to seeing his old teachers, and he was sure they would be surprised about how successful he had become.

William was not a model high school student. In fact, he was awful! His guidance counselor, Ms. Lewis, always told him that she couldn't understand how someone as bright as he was could get such poor grades. William came very close to failing at least three of his subjects every marking period. He especially disliked math and science.

After school on Wednesdays, Thursdays, and Fridays, William would get into his old Honda Civic and drive to Cedar Street, where he worked the afternoon shift at Milton's Bookstore. This was his favorite place to be. He loved being surrounded by books, and when he wasn't helping customers, he would sit behind the counter and read as much as he could. During these afternoon shifts, William read some books that changed his life. One of his favorites was *On the Road* by Jack Kerouac. His reading inspired him to keep a journal, which he wrote in every day.

When it was time to consider college, William spent many hours with Ms. Lewis thinking about his future. After reading his journals, Ms. Lewis suggested that perhaps William would be happiest at a college where he could study creative writing. The rest is history!

William was one of the top students in the Creative Writing Program at the University of Wisconsin. During his junior year, one of his essays was accepted for publication in a national magazine, and soon after that, William received a call from an editor at Bound Brook Publishing who wanted to publish a collection of William's short stories. As soon as the book was published, William sent a copy to Ms. Lewis thanking her for her support and advice.

Now he was on his way back to visit Ms. Lewis and his other teachers, who were probably all asking the same question. Can this be the same William Reese?

▶ Rules for Using Periods

- Use a period after an initial and after every part of an abbreviation, unless the abbreviation has become an acronym—an abbreviation that is pronounced as a word, such as AIDS—or a widely recognized name (TV, FBI, NATO, NASA). Titles—Mr., Ms., Dr., and so on—are also abbreviations that use periods. If the abbreviation comes at the end of a sentence, only one period is needed.

  Examples:

  The tour leaves on **Mon., Jan. 1, at 3 P.M.**

  The book was written by **C.S.** Lewis.

  A.J. Mandelli researched brain function for the **FBI.**

- Use a period before a decimal and between dollars and cents.

  Examples:

  A gallon equals **3.875** liters.

  The new textbook costs **$54.75.**

  Only **5.6** percent of our consumers spend over **$100.00** per month on our products.

- Use a period at the end of a sentence that makes a statement.

  Examples:

  Henry Kissinger served under two U.S. presidents.

  Wilson will lecture in the forum after school today.

  Many consider P.T. Barnum the best salesman ever to have walked the Earth.

- Use a period at the end of a sentence that makes a request, gives an instruction, or states a command.

  Examples:

  Empty the kitchen trash before you take the garbage out.

  Turn right at the first stop light, and then go to the second house on the left.

- Use a period at the end of a sentence that asks an indirect question.

  Examples:

  My neighbor asked if we had seen his cat. (The direct question was, "Have you seen my cat?")

  Quentin wanted to know how we had arrived at that answer. (The direct question was, "How did you arrive at that answer?")

Practice

Choose the correctly written version from each of the following sets of sentences. You will find the answers to each set of questions at the end of the lesson.

1. **a.** The train passed through Rockford, Ill., on its way to St. Joseph, Mo.
   b. The train passed through Rockford, Ill, on its way to St Joseph, Mo.
   c. The train passed through Rockford, Ill, on its way to St. Joseph, Mo.

2. **a.** Ms Cory Ames, Dr Matthew Olson, and H.J. Lane went to Chicago, Ill..
   b. Ms Cory Ames, Dr Matthew Olson, and HJ Lane went to Chicago, Ill.
   c. Ms. Cory Ames, Dr. Matthew Olson, and H.J. Lane went to Chicago, Ill.

3. **a.** The bedrooms measured 12 ft. by 14 ft.
   b. The bedrooms measured 12 ft by 14 ft.
   c. The bedrooms measured 12 ft. by 14 ft..

4. **a.** Bob asked if the price of the CD was $13.98?
   b. Bob asked if the price of the CD was $13.98.
   c. Bob asked if the price of the CD was $1398¢.

5. **a.** Tie your shoe. Before you trip and break a leg.
   b. Tie your shoe before you trip and break a leg.
   c. Tie your shoe before you trip and break a leg

6. a. Mr and Mrs Fletcher visited ten cities in 20 days.
b. Mr. and Mrs. Fletcher visited ten cities in 20 days.
c. Mr and Mrs. Fletcher visited ten cities in 20 days.

7. a. Mayor and Mrs. Dorian will address the city council at 8:00 PM
b. Mayor and Mrs Dorian will address the city council at 8:00 P.M.
c. Mayor and Mrs. Dorian will address the city council at 8:00 P.M.

8. a. Oh, all right. Tell me your riddle.
b. Oh. all right. Tell me your riddle.
c. Oh, all right Tell me your riddle.

▶ Rules for Using Question Marks and Exclamation Points

- Use a question mark after a word or group of words that asks a question, even if it is not a complete sentence.
  Examples:
  What did you do last night?
  Will you put out the trash?
  Okay?
  May we go to the movies after we've finished our homework?
  Are we?
- Use an exclamation point after a sentence that expresses strong feeling.
  Examples:
  Look out for that car!
  I just can't stand the smell in here!

A word of caution about using exclamation points to show strong feeling: Exclamation points are a little bit like salt on food. Most people like a little bit. Nobody likes too much.

- Use an exclamation point after an interjection—a word or phrase expressing strong feeling—when it is written as a single sentence.
  Examples:
  Doggone it!
  Yikes!
- Use an exclamation point after a sentence that begins with a question word but doesn't ask a question.
  Examples:
  What a dunce I am!
  How marvelous of you to come!

Practice
Choose the correctly written version of each of the following sets of sentences.

9. a. Help! I'm falling?
b. Help! I'm falling.
c. Help! I'm falling!

10. a. I can't believe how naive I was!
b. I can't believe how naive I was.
c. I can't believe how naive I was?

11. a. The auditor asked me why I didn't save the receipts?
b. The auditor asked me why I didn't save the receipts.
c. The auditor asked me why I didn't save the receipts!

12. a. Can you tell me the seating capacity of this meeting room.
b. Can you tell me the seating capacity of this meeting room?
c. Can you tell me the seating capacity of this meeting room!

13. a. How utterly disgusting this movie is.
b. How utterly disgusting this movie is?
c. How utterly disgusting this movie is!

14. **a.** Was Alexander the Great born in 350 B.C.
  b. Was Alexander the great born in 350 B.C.?
  c. Was Alexander the Great born in 350 B.C.?

15. **a.** Our group will meet at the library at 10:00
    P.M. to research T.S. Eliot.
  b. Our group will meet at the library at 10:00 PM
    to research T.S. Eliot.
  c. Our group will meet at the library at 10:00 P.M.
    to research TS. Eliot.

16. **a.** Is this sweater $59.95 or $69.95?
  b. Is this sweater $59.95 or $69.95.
  c. Is this sweater $5995 or $6995!

17. **a.** Wow. What a close call that was?
  b. Wow! What a close call that was.
  c. Wow! What a close call that was!

18. **a.** Those carpenters. Do you know how much
    they charged?
  b. Those carpenters? Do you know how much
    they charged?
  c. Those carpenters! Do you know how much
    they charged?

▶ **Answers**

1. a.
2. c.
3. a.
4. b.
5. b.
6. b.
7. c.
8. a.
9. c.
10. a.
11. b.
12. b.
13. c.
14. c.
15. a.
16. a.
17. c.
18. c.

Skill Building until Next Time

Take a few minutes to practice what you have learned today. If you are reading a book right now, look through a few of the pages until you find at least three examples of each type of endmark you learned about today. Are the endmarks used according to the rules you used today? If you're not currently reading a book, just grab one from the shelf at home or at work.

3 ▶ Avoiding Faulty Sentences

LESSON SUMMARY

This lesson will help you distinguish between complete sentences and faulty sentences so that you can avoid writing sentence fragments, run-on sentences, and comma splices.

egin your study of complete sentences by looking at the **Problem** paragraph that appears on the next page. Underline the groups of words that form complete sentences. See if you can distinguish them from the fragments, run-ons, and comma splices included in the paragraph. Then check your work against the **Solution** paragraph, also on the next page, where the complete sentences are underlined.

Problem

Just the other day, I came home from work as excited as I had ever been. The night before, someone from Publisher's Clearinghouse had called. To tell me that I would be receiving a prize package worth potentially millions of dollars. I was so excited because, unlike other offers, this really sounded legitimate, it sounded to me as though I might really win something this time. I hastily opened the mailbox. Hoping to find the promised envelope. There it was. Between the *Life* magazine and the Fingerhut catalog. The promised letter. When I finally finished reading the entire mailing. I realized my chances were really no better with this contest than they had been for any other contest I had entered in the past and I was disappointed that I had spent so much time reading all of the material then I threw it all in the recycling basket and went to bed. Dejected.

Solution

<u>Just the other day, I came home from work as excited as I had ever been.</u> <u>The night before, someone from Publisher's Clearinghouse had called.</u> To tell me that I would be receiving a prize package worth potentially millions of dollars. I was so excited because, unlike other offers, this really sounded legitimate, it sounded to me as though I might really win something this time. <u>I hastily opened the mailbox.</u> Hoping to find the promised envelope. <u>There it was.</u> Between the *Life* magazine and the Fingerhut catalog. The promised letter. When I finally finished reading the entire mailing. I realized my chances were really no better with this contest than they had been for any other contest I had entered in the past and I was disappointed that I had spent so much time reading all of the material then I threw it all in the recycling basket and went to bed. Dejected.

▶ Complete Sentences

A complete sentence is a group of words that meets **all** three of the following criteria:

1. It has a verb (a word or phrase that explains an action such as *want, run, take, give,* or a state of being, such as *am, is, are, was, were, be*). Many sentences have more than one verb. The verbs in the following sentences are highlighted for you.

   Examples:
   > Bob and Alexandra both **want** a promotion. (action verb)
   > Yurika **drafted** a memo and **sent** it to the sales department. (action verbs)
   > Herbert and Tan **are** the chief operators in this department. (state of being verb)

2. It has a subject (someone or something that performs the action or serves as the main focus of the sentence). As with verbs, many sentences have more than one subject.

   Examples:
   > **Bob** and **Alexandra** both want a promotion.
   > **Yurika** drafted a memo and sent it to the sales department.
   > **Herbert** and **Tan** are the chief operators in this department.

3. It expresses a complete thought. In other words, the group of words has a completed meaning. Sometimes, a group of words has both a subject and a verb but still does not express a complete thought. Look at the following examples. The subjects and verbs are highlighted to make them easier to identify.

Complete sentences (also called independent clauses):

> **I left** an hour earlier than usual.
>
> Our **team finished** its year-end evaluation.
>
> **Roger tried** to explain his position.

Sentence fragments (dependent clauses):

> If **I left** an hour earlier than usual.
>
> When our **team finished** its year-end evaluation.
>
> Whenever **Roger tried** to explain his position.

▶ Sentence Fragments

In the last set of examples, you may have noticed that each fragment is longer than the similar complete sentence. The groups of words are otherwise the same, but the fragments have an extra word at the beginning. These words are called *subordinating conjunctions*. If a group of words that would normally be a complete sentence is preceded by a subordinating conjunction, you need something more to complete the thought. These *subordinate* or *dependent clauses* need something more to complete their meaning; therefore, they *depend* on an *independent clause*, a group of words that by itself could form a complete sentence. Examine how the fragments have been rewritten here to express a complete thought.

> If I left an hour earlier than usual, I would be able to avoid rush hour.
>
> When our team finished its year-end evaluation, we all took the next day off.
>
> Whenever Roger tried to explain his position, he misquoted the facts.

These words can be used as subordinating conjunctions:

after	once	until
although	since	when
as	than	whenever
because	that	where
before	though	wherever
if	unless	while

Sometimes, a subordinating conjunction is a phrase rather than a single word:

> **as if** we didn't already know
>
> **as though** she had always lived in the town
>
> **as long as** they can still be heard
>
> **as soon as** I can finish my work
>
> **even though** you aren't quite ready
>
> **in order to** proceed more carefully
>
> **so that** all of us understand exactly

Subordinate clauses used as sentences are only one type of sentence fragment. Look at the questions in the table that follows. For each question, choose the group of words that forms a complete sentence and put the corresponding letter in the box at the right. See if you notice any similarities among the groups of words that are fragments.

WORD GROUP A	WORD GROUP B	?
1. We are ready for the next task.	Washing the car.	☐
2. Seeing the plane arriving.	Heather's family rushed to the gate.	☐
3. Broken after years of use.	The receptionist finally got a new phone.	☐
4. We saw Andrea sitting all by herself.	Imagining what Florida was like in March.	☐

The complete sentences are 1. A, 2. B, 3. B, and 4. A. The fragments are simply phrases. They do not contain a subject or a verb. If you combine the two sets of words, both will be part of a complete sentence. See how this is done in the following examples. With some of the sentences, all you need is a comma. With others, you must add a few extra words to incorporate the phrase into the rest of the sentence.

1. We are ready for the next task, which is washing the car.
2. Seeing the plane arriving, Heather's family rushed to the gate.

3. Since the phone was broken after years of use, the receptionist finally got a new one.
4. We saw Andrea sitting all by herself, imagining what Florida was like in March.

Now look at this table. In each set, one of the options is a complete sentence. The other is a fragment. Put the letter of the complete sentences in the box at the far right. See if you notice any similarities among the fragments.

WORD GROUP A	WORD GROUP B	?
1. About the way he combs his hair.	I've noticed something very strange.	☐
2. My aunt is a respiratory therapist.	A person who helps people rebuild their lungs and circulatory system.	☐
3. Benjamin saw a piece of key lime pie.	His favorite type of dessert.	☐
4. And tried to sell popcorn and candy.	We went door to door.	☐
5. During the rest of the afternoon.	Everything went smoothly.	☐
6. Icy roads and hazardous weather.	We couldn't make the deadline.	☐
7. In the parking ramp near our building.	I was fortunate to find a parking spot.	☐
8. And saw the picture of our company's new owner.	We read the morning paper.	☐
9. We traveled through the desert all night.	Without seeing a single car or building.	☐
10. We walked all over downtown.	And applied for part-time jobs at theaters.	☐

The complete sentences are 1. B, 2. A, 3. A, 4. B, 5. B, 6. B, 7. B, 8. B, 9. A, and 10. A.

Most of the fragments are phrases that can easily be incorporated into a complete sentence using the independent clause with which they are paired. Try to do this yourself. Compare your sentences with the versions that follow.

Look at sentences 1, 5, 7, and 9. The fragments in these sentences were nothing more than phrases separated from the independent clauses. All you need to do is add the fragment to the complete sentence in a spot where it fits. No punctuation or additional words are needed.

1. I've noticed something very strange about the way he combs his hair.
5. Everything went smoothly during the rest of the afternoon.
7. I was fortunate to find a spot in the parking ramp near our building.
9. We traveled through the desert all night without seeing a single car or building.

Now examine sentences 2 and 3. These fragments are phrases that explain or further identify something in the complete sentence. Such phrases are called *appositive* phrases. All you need to do is place a comma after the word being explained or identified, and then add the appositive phrase.

2. My aunt is a respiratory therapist, a person who helps people rebuild their lungs and respiratory system.
3. Benjamin saw key lime pie, his favorite type of dessert.

Take a look at sentences 4, 8, and 10. In these sentences, the fragment is a verb (action) separated from the independent clause or the complete sentence. All that is required is to add the fragment to the sentence.

4. We went door to door and tried to sell popcorn and candy.
8. We read the morning paper and saw the picture of our company's new owner.
10. We walked all over downtown and applied for part-time jobs at theaters.

Finally, look at the remaining sentence, 6. In this sentence, extra words are needed to add the fragment to the sentence.

6. We couldn't make the deadline because of the icy roads and hazardous weather.

▶ Run-On Sentences

An *independent clause* is a group of words that could be a complete sentence all by itself. A *run-on sentence* is one in which independent clauses have been run together without punctuation (a period, semicolon, or comma).

Examples:

Lynn moved from Minneapolis her job was transferred.

The concert seemed unending it lasted almost until midnight.

We got some gas then we headed off to Omaha.

All three examples can be corrected quite easily in one of three ways:

1. By adding a period and a capital letter.

Lynn moved from Minneapolis. Her job was transferred.

The concert seemed unending. It lasted almost until midnight.

We got some gas. Then we headed off to Omaha.

2. By adding a comma and a conjunction (*and, but, or, for, nor, yet, so*). Sometimes, you have to change the order of the words.

Lynn's job was transferred, so she moved from Minneapolis.

The concert seemed unending, for it lasted almost until midnight.

We got some gas, and then we headed off to Omaha.

3. By turning one of the independent clauses into a dependent clause. To do this, you need to add a subordinating conjunction where it fits in the sentence. This can usually be done in two different ways: by rewording the clauses or by using different subordinating conjunctions. Remember the list of subordinating conjunction you saw earlier in this lesson?

Lynn moved from Minneapolis because her job was transferred.

When her job was transferred, Lynn moved from Minneapolis.

Since the concert lasted almost until midnight, it seemed unending.

The concert seemed unending because it lasted until almost midnight.

After we got some gas, we headed off to Omaha.

We headed off to Omaha after we got some gas.

Practice

Choose the answers that include *only* complete sentences. Watch for fragments as well as run-ons. Answers are at the end of the lesson.

1. **a.** The puppy chewed on everything. And ruined my favorite shoes.
   b. The puppy chewed on everything and ruined my favorite shoes.

2. **a.** Julie is a loyal friend. She helps whenever she is needed.
   b. Julie is a loyal friend she helps whenever she is needed.

3. **a.** The car was in the garage we thought you were home.
   b. The car was in the garage. We thought you were home.

4. a. Lisa lost five pounds. After only one week on the new diet.
   b. Lisa lost five pounds after only one week on the new diet.

5. a. You can register for the class in the office on the second floor.
   b. You can register for the class. In the office on the second floor.

6. a. Samantha needs a few more days to finish the report it is more involved than she anticipated.
   b. Samantha needs a few more days to finish the report. It is more involved than she anticipated.

7. a. After Marsha used the milk, Stan went to the supermarket.
   b. Marsha used the milk Stan went to the supermarket.

8. a. Tanya completed the form she gave it to the receptionist.
   b. Tanya completed the form, and she gave it to the receptionist.

9. a. Louis was eager to see the dentist his toothache was getting worse.
   b. Louis was eager to see the dentist. His toothache was getting worse.

10. a. Jenny looked for a bank that offered better interest rates.
   b. Jenny looked for a bank. Offered better interest rates.

▶ Comma Splices

A *comma splice* is the last kind of sentence fault you will study today. It is actually a special type of run-on sentence in which a comma is used in place of a semicolon to join two independent clauses without a conjunction. A comma splice can be corrected by putting a semicolon in place of the comma or by adding a conjunction after the comma.

Wrong:
   Henry lives across the street, he has been there for 25 years.
Correct:
   Henry lives across the street; he has been there for 25 years.
   Henry lives across the street, and he has been there for 25 years.
Wrong:
   Mary heads the search committee, John is the recorder.
Correct:
   Mary heads the search committee; John is the recorder.
   Mary heads the search committee, and John is the recorder.
Wrong:
   Sid gave demonstrations all summer long, he returned in the fall.
Correct:
   Sid gave demonstrations all summer long; he returned in the fall.
   Sid gave demonstrations all summer long, but he returned in the fall.

Practice

Here is an opportunity to apply what you have learned about complete sentences, fragments, run-ons, and comma splices. In each of the following numbered items, decide whether the group of words is a correctly written sentence or sentences (S), a fragment (F), a run-on sentence (ROS), or a comma splice (CS). Write the label next to each number, and then check your work against the answer key at the end of the lesson. You may recognize some of these sentences from the opening example paragraph. By now, you know how to correct the ones that were not complete sentences.

11. Dr. Anders left detailed care instructions for the patient. A personal friend of his.

12. The night before, someone from Publisher's Clearinghouse had called. To tell me that I would be receiving a prize package worth potentially millions of dollars.

13. I was so excited because unlike the other offers, this really sounded legitimate, it sounded to me as though I might really win something this time.

14. I hastily opened the mailbox. Hoping to find the promised envelope.

15. There it was. The promised letter.

16. When I finally finished reading the entire mailing.

17. The officer responded to the call, he received it at 8:10 P.M.

18. Emily posted the last transaction it was time to close the books for the day.

19. Our new computer system is still not working properly.

20. Hanging over the doorway in the office next to the conference room.

Rewrite the fragments, run-ons, and comma splices as complete sentences in the space below.

_____

_____

_____

_____

_____

_____

_____

_____

_____

_____

_____

_____

_____

_____

_____

_____

_____

_____

_____

_____

▶ Answers

1. b.		**11.** F
2. a.		**12.** F
3. b.		**13.** CS
4. b.		**14.** F
5. a.		**15.** F
6. b.		**16.** F
7. a.		**17.** CS
8. b.		**18.** ROS
9. b.		**19.** S
10. a.		**20.** F

Skill Building until Next Time

Go back to the paragraph at the beginning of the lesson. Revise it to eliminate the sentence fragments, comma splices, and run-on sentences. As you read the morning paper or written material at work, look for sentence faults. If you find none, look for complete sentences that could be combined. Chances are, you'll find plenty of those in a newspaper. You can also find plenty of sentence faults, especially fragments, in advertisements. Practice writing complete sentences in any written work you are assigned.

▶ Commas and Sentence Parts

LESSON SUMMARY

Lessons 4 and 5 deal with commas. Today's lesson is about how commas relate to the parts of sentences, such as clauses and phrases.

uring this lesson, you will learn how to use commas in relationship to sentence parts. As you progress through this lesson, remember what you have learned about sentences and sentence faults in Lesson 3. Before you begin this lesson, see how much you already know about commas and sentence parts. Insert commas where you think they should be in the **Problem** version of the sentences that appear on the next page. Check yourself against the corrected version of the sentences in the **Solution** section that follows.

PROBLEM	SOLUTION
Worried I tried to reach him on the phone again.	Worried, I tried to reach him on the phone again.
Before setting up the computer Kayla read all the instruction booklets carefully.	Before setting up the computer, Kayla read all the instruction booklets carefully.
As soon as the paint dries we can apply another coat.	As soon as the paint dries, we can apply another coat.
Thinking carefully about the requests of his coworkers Jason scheduled a meeting with his boss.	Thinking carefully about the requests of his coworkers, Jason scheduled a meeting with his boss.
Like an excited child Jan tore open the wrapping paper to see her gift.	Like an excited child, Jan tore open the wrapping paper to see her gift.
Because tulips need a great deal of sunlight to grow we decided to plant a different kind of flower in our shady backyard.	Because tulips need a great deal of sunlight to grow, we decided to plant a different kind of flower in our shady backyard.
Mark spent more than three hours brainstorming with the other supervisors who are always very receptive to his ideas.	Mark spent more than three hours brainstorming with the other supervisors, who are always very receptive to his ideas.
Jill Johnson the newest member of the human resources staff has more than ten years of experience in the field.	Jill Johnson, the newest member of the human resources staff, has more than ten years of experience in the field.
The workshop which I will attend is scheduled for the last Friday of the month.	The workshop, which I will attend, is scheduled for the for the last Friday of the month.

► Commas Following Introductory Words, Phrases, and Clauses

Use a comma to set off introductory words, phrases, and clauses from the main part of a sentence. The comma keeps a reader from accidentally attaching the introductory portion to the main part of the sentence and having to go back and reread the sentence. In other words, commas following introductory elements will save the reader time and reduce the chances of misinterpreting what you write. Examine the following examples to see how introductory words, phrases, and clauses are set off with commas.

Words:
>   Disappointed, we left the movie before it ended.
>   Annoyed, the manager stomped back into the storeroom.
>   Amazed, Captain Holland dismissed the rest of the troops.

Phrases:

> Expecting the worst, we liquidated most of our inventory.

> Badly injured in the accident, the president was gone for two months.

> Reluctant to make matters any worse, the doctor called in a specialist.

Clauses:

> If we plan carefully for the grand opening, we can increase sales.

> While we were eating lunch, an important fax came.

> Because we left before the meeting ended, we were not eligible to win a door prize.

Remember the fragment section of Lesson 3? Part of it dealt with subordinate or dependent clauses. Subordinate or dependent clauses are what you see in the last set of examples above. The first part of each sentence, the subordinate or dependent clause, is followed by a comma. The two parts of each of these sentences could very easily be reversed and the sentence would still make sense. However, if you reverse the sentence parts, making the independent clause the first clause in the sentence, you would NOT need a comma.

Subordinate clauses *after* the independent clause:

> We can increase sales if we plan carefully for the grand opening.

> An important fax came while we were eating lunch.

> We were not eligible to win a door prize because we left before the meeting ended.

Practice

Choose the correctly written sentence from each of the following pairs. Answers are provided at the end of the lesson.

1. a. Content for the first time in his life, Bryce returned to school.
   b. Content for the first time in his life Bryce returned to school.

2. a. As far as I'm concerned we can call this project a success.
   b. As far as I'm concerned, we can call this project a success.

3. a. I will never forget this moment, as long as I live.
   b. I will never forget this moment as long as I live.

4. a. By the time we finally made up our minds, the contract had been awarded to someone else.
   b. By the time we finally made up our minds the contract had been awarded to someone else.

5. a. Indignant, Mr. Caster left the restaurant without leaving a tip.
   b. Indignant Mr. Caster left the restaurant without leaving a tip.

6. a. Wayne was delighted when he found out he'd been awarded the leading role in the show.
   b. Wayne was delighted, when he found out he'd been awarded the leading role in the show.

7. a. By designing the program ourselves, we saved a great deal of expense.
   b. By designing the program ourselves we saved a great deal of expense.

8. a. I began working for this company, before I was sixteen.

b. Before I was sixteen, I began working for this company.

9. a. Dripping with water from head to toe, Angie climbed the bank of the river.

b. Dripping with water from head to toe Angie climbed the bank of the river.

10. a. The company honored its oldest employee at the annual meeting.

b. The company honored its oldest employee, at the annual meeting.

Commas help a reader know which words belong together. Add commas to the following sentences to help make their meaning clear.

1. Inside the house was clean and tastefully decorated.
2. After running the greyhounds settled back into their boxes.
3. Alone at night time seems endless.
4. As he watched the game slowly came to an end.

You should have marked the sentences like this:

1. Inside, the house was clean and tastefully decorated.
2. After running, the greyhounds settled back into their boxes.
3. Alone at night, time seems endless.
4. As he watched, the game slowly came to an end.

▶ Commas with Appositives

An *appositive* is a word or group of words that immediately follows a noun or pronoun. The appositive makes the noun or pronoun clearer or more definite by explaining or identifying it. Look at the examples below. The appositives and appositive phrases have been highlighted.

Examples:

Rachel Stein won the first prize, **an expense-paid vacation to the Bahamas.**

New Orleans, **home of the Saints**, is one of my favorite cities.

One of the most inspiring motivators in college basketball is Dr. Tom Davis, **coach of the Iowa Hawkeyes.**

Sometimes, a proper name that identifies or further explains will follow a noun or pronoun. Although this is also a type of appositive, it is not set off by commas.

Examples:

My sister **Deb** lives four hours away.

The noted novelist **Barbara Kingsolver** writes about the South and Southwest.

The president **Manuel Diaz** will visit this site tomorrow.

Place commas where they are needed in the following sentences.

1. Ms. Mason the bank manager scheduled a meeting with new employees.
2. MP3 players devices virtually unheard of a decade ago are very common today.
3. Maggie loves to take long walks on the nature trail an oasis of calm.
4. Healthcare coverage a major consideration for everyone has steadily worsened over the years.
5. The poem was written by Sylvia Plath a very accomplished poet.
6. My friend Cynthia threw me a surprise party last year.

You should have marked the sentences like this:

1. Ms. Mason, the bank manager, scheduled a meeting with new employees.
2. MP3 players, devices virtually unheard of a decade ago, are very common today.
3. Maggie loves to take long walks on the nature trail, an oasis of calm.
4. Healthcare coverage, a major consideration for everyone, has steadily worsened over the years.
5. The poem was written by Sylvia Plath, a very accomplished poet.
6. My friend Cynthia threw me a surprise party last year. (no comma needed)

▶ Commas and Nonrestrictive Clauses

Earlier in this lesson, you learned that a subordinate clause at the beginning of a sentence is followed by a comma, but a subordinate clause any other place in the sentence is not set off by a comma. This is true only if the clause is an essential clause. In some sentences, a clause cannot be omitted without changing the basic meaning of the sentences. Omitting such a clause changes the meaning of the sentence or makes it untrue. Such a clause is called an *essential* or *restrictive* clause.

Example:
All drivers **who have had a drunk driving conviction** should have their licenses revoked.
All drivers should have their licenses revoked.

The highlighted clause is essential because the meaning of the sentence is changed drastically if the clause is removed from the sentence. A restrictive clause is not set off with commas.

However, a *nonessential* or *nonrestrictive* clause must to be set off by commas. A clause is nonrestrictive if it simply adds information that is not essential to the basic meaning of the sentence. If a nonrestrictive clause is removed, the basic meaning of the sentence is not changed.

Example:
My father, **who is still farming**, is 74 years old.
My father is 74 years old.

The highlighted clause is nonrestrictive. If it is removed from the sentence, the basic meaning of the sentence is not changed. Nonrestrictive clauses usually begin with one of these subordinating conjunctions: *who, whom, whose, which,* or *that.* (Technically, the proper subordinating conjunction for a restrictive clause is *that,* while nonrestrictive clauses use *which,* but in practice, many writers ignore this distinction.)

Practice

Each of the following sentences contains a subordinate clause. These are highlighted for you. If the clause is restrictive, or essential, write R in the box at the right. If the clause is nonrestrictive, or nonessential, put N in the box and set the clause off with commas. Answers are at the end of the lesson.

11. Matt **who loves to play video games** is interested in a computer science career. □

12. My grandfather **who was born in Berlin** speaks with a German accent. □

13. James **who is very shy** had a great deal of trouble with his first speech. □

14. The hotel pays the parking ramp fees for anyone **who is a registered guest.** □

15. People **who are born on February 29** grow old more slowly than the rest of us. □

16. Animals **that have backbones** are called vertebrates. □

17. Nicotine **which is present in tobacco products** is a powerful poison. □

18. Many Scandinavian names end with *sen* or *son* **both of which mean *son of*.** □

19. We live on Fleur Drive **which is right next to the airport.** □

20. Mrs. Olson is not a teacher **who takes homework lightly.** □

► Review

This next exercise reviews everything you have learned so far. This passage contains no commas, endmarks, or capitalization. Use what you have learned to add capitalization, endmarks, and commas to make sense of the **Problem** version of the passage. Check your work against the **Solution** version that follows.

Problem

even though peter liked his job a great deal he always looked forward to his summer vacation it was the highlight of his year usually he spent two weeks in the middle of july at camp wi wi ta which was forty miles from his home he was responsible for six physically challenged children for 24 hours a day for two weeks how he loved camp

peter took the counseling job one he loved dearly very seriously each morning he rose before the first child awoke and never went to bed until the last of his kids went to sleep at night the best part of the job was challenging the kids to do things for themselves peter would insist that they comb their hair or cut their own food even if they begged for help the camp dean and some of the other counselors thought peter was slacking on the job but he didn't see it that way he enjoyed knowing that his kids left camp more capable and confident than they had been when they arrived

Solution

Even though Peter liked his job a great deal, he always looked forward to his summer vacation. It was the highlight of his year. Usually, he spent two weeks in the middle of July at Camp Wi Wi Ta, which was forty miles from his home. He was responsible for six physically challenged children for 24 hours a day for two weeks. How he loved camp!

Peter took the counseling job, one he loved dearly, very seriously. Each morning, he rose before the first child awoke and never went to bed until the last of his kids went to sleep at night. The best part of the job was challenging the kids to do things for themselves. Peter would insist that they comb their hair or cut their own food even if they begged for help. The camp dean and some of the other counselors thought Peter was slacking on the job, but he didn't see it that way. He enjoyed knowing that his kids left camp more capable and confident than they had been when they arrived.

► Answers

1. a.
2. b.
3. b.
4. a.
5. a.
6. a.
7. a.
8. b.
9. a.
10. a.
11. N. Matt, who loves to play video games, is interested in a computer science career.
12. N. My grandfather, who was born in Berlin, speaks with a German accent.

13. N. James, who is very shy, had a great deal of trouble with his first speech.
14. R. No commas are needed.
15. R. No commas are needed.
16. R. No commas are needed.
17. N. Nicotine, which is present in tobacco products, is a powerful poison.
18. N. Many Scandinavian names end with *son* or *sen*, both of which mean *son of.*
19. N. We live on Fleur Drive, which is right next to the airport.
20. R. No commas are needed.

Skill Building until Next Time

As you've seen in this lesson, omitting commas before introductory elements or wrongly placing commas around restrictive clauses can lead to humorous misreadings. Write some sentences of your own that are hard to read without commas, like this: "As they ate the horse moved closer." Then correct them by adding commas.

5 ▶ Commas That Separate

LESSON SUMMARY
Besides setting off sentence parts, commas are used in many other situations. This lesson reviews the many instances in which you should use commas to separate sentence elements.

ommas are used to separate or clarify relationships between sentence parts to make the meaning of a sentence clear and easy to grasp. In this lesson, you'll learn how to use commas to separate independent clauses, items in a series, items in a date or address, two or more adjectives preceding a noun, and contrasting elements and words that interrupt the flow of thought in a sentence. The last section of the lesson explains how to use commas in the greetings and closings of a friendly letter.

Begin by seeing how much you already know about commas that separate. Add commas where you think they are needed to the **Problem** column on the next page. Check yourself against the corrected version in the **Solution** column. Try to identify the rules that apply to those you missed as you go through the lesson.

Problem

Dear Ms. Ames

I want to thank you for writing the recommendation letter a very kind gesture. I also wanted to tell you that Mr. Matthews the director of the camp offered me the counselor job. I will work at Camp Arrowhead in June July and August. Additionally I will accompany the campers on a week-long trip to Hershey Pennsylvania.

I will have many responsibilities at the camp but most of my time will be spent organizing the sports activities. I will be teaching the campers to play soccer basketball and tennis all sports that I happen to love. Louise who directs the sports program at Camp Arrowhead is an accomplished athlete with a dynamic personality. I am looking forward to working with her.

Ms. Ames I am so grateful for all your support. Without your guidance as well as your confidence in me I wouldn't have received this job offer. When I begin my summer job I will be ready to make an excellent impression an eager and well-prepared young woman. This summer thanks to you will be one that I will never forget.

By the way you can write to me at Camp Arrowhead 303 Valley Road Lebanon Pennsylvania.

Sincerely,

Solution

Dear Ms. Ames,

I want to thank you for writing the recommendation letter, a very kind gesture. I also wanted to tell you that Mr. Matthews, the director of the camp, offered me the counselor job. I will work at Camp Arrowhead in June, July, and August. Additionally, I will accompany the campers on a week-long trip to Hershey, Pennsylvania.

I will have many responsibilities at the camp, but most of my time will be spent organizing the sports activities. I will be teaching the campers to play soccer, basketball, and tennis, all sports that I happen to love. Louise, who directs the sports program at Camp Arrowhead, is an accomplished athlete with a dynamic personality. I am looking forward to working with her.

Ms. Ames, I am so grateful for all your support. Without your guidance, as well as your confidence in me, I wouldn't have received this job offer. When I begin my summer job, I will be ready to make an excellent impression, an eager and well-prepared young woman. This summer, thanks to you, will be one that I will never forget.

By the way, you can write to me at Camp Arrowhead, 303 Valley Road, Lebanon, Pennsylvania.

Sincerely,

▶ Commas with Independent Clauses Joined by a Conjunction

As you may recall from Lesson 3, an *independent clause* is a group of words that could stand alone as a complete sentence. A *conjunction* is a joining word: *and, but, or, for, nor, so,* or *yet.* Sometimes, a writer will combine two or more independent clauses to form a compound sentence. If a conjunction joins the clauses, place a comma after the first clause. The commas and conjunctions are highlighted in the following examples.

Examples:

I went to bed early last night, **so** I felt rested this morning.

The city's economic situation has improved, **but** there are still neighborhoods where many people depend on the generosity of others in order to live.

Susan worked through lunch, **and** now she is able to leave the office early.

If independent clauses are joined *without* a conjunction, they are separated by a semicolon instead of a comma.

Examples:

> I went to bed early last night; I felt rested this morning.
>
> The city's economic situation has improved; however, there are still neighborhoods where many people depend on the generosity of others in order to live.
>
> Susan worked through lunch; now she is able to leave the office early.

Practice

Use commas and semicolons to correctly punctuate the following sentences. Answers are at the end of the lesson.

1. You can safely view an eclipse through the viewing glass of a welding helmet or you can look through a piece of overexposed film.

2. The prisoner showed no remorse as the guilty verdict was announced nor did the tears of the victim's family arouse any emotion.

3. The young calf put its head over the fence and it licked my hand.

4. Icebergs in the Antarctic are flat and smooth but those in the Arctic are rough.

5. I understand your position on this issue I still believe you are dead wrong.

6. I like Sam he likes me for we are best of friends.

7. The inventory is valued at one million dollars but it's not enough to cover our debt.

8. If you know of anyone with data processing experience encourage him or her to apply for this new position.

► Commas to Separate Items in a Series

Commas are used to separate items in lists of similar words, phrases, or clauses to make the material easier for a reader to understand. The last item in a series is also usually preceded by a conjunction. Strictly speaking, no comma is needed before the conjunction. (However, many writers—some test writers included—prefer to use a comma before the final conjunction to avoid confusion.)

Examples:

> Al, Jane, Herbert, and Willis all applied for the promotion.
>
> The old Tempo's engine squealed loudly, shook violently, and came to a halt.
>
> The instructions clearly showed how to assemble the equipment, how to load the software, and how to boot the system.

If each item in the series is separated by a conjunction, no commas are needed.

Example:

> Billie and Charles and Cameron performed at the company Christmas party.

► Commas to Separate Items in a Date or an Address

When giving a complete date in the format *month-day-year*, put a comma on either side of the year. When giving a date that is only a month and year, no comma is needed.

Use a comma to separate each element of an address, such as the street address, city, state, and country. A comma is also used after the state or country if the sentence continues after the address.

Examples:
> We moved from Fayetteville, North Carolina, on May 16, 2005.
> Since November 1994, Terry has lived at 654 36th Street, Lincoln, Nebraska.
> Dwana attended Drake University, Des Moines, Iowa, both fall 2004 and spring 2005.

Practice

Add commas and endmarks where they are needed to the following sentences. Use not only what you are learning in this lesson but also what you learned in Lesson 4. Answers appear at the end of the lesson.

9. After he ran into the mayor's car with his truck Adam used his cell phone to call the police his doctor lawyer and insurance agent.

10. The homegrown philosopher who lives next door at 251 Acorn Street Libertyville Kansas claims to know exactly who invented the wheel sliced bread and kissing.

11. Estelle was born on January 31 1953 and Arun was born on June 30 1960.

12. Looking for a solution to the printing problem Karissa asked an older employee questioned the supervisor and finally consulted the printer manual.

13. Baruch brought a jello salad to the potluck Shannon brought peanuts M&M's mints and pretzels.

▶ Commas to Separate Adjectives

Use commas to separate two or more equally important adjectives.

Examples:
> Alex avoided the **friendly, talkative, pleasant** boy sitting next to him at school.
> The carpenter repaired the floor with **dark, aged, oak** flooring.
> The reporter spoke with several **intense, talented** high school athletes.

Pay close attention to the last sentence. You'll notice that the words *several*, *high*, and *school* are also adjectives modifying *athletes*. Not all adjectives modifying the same word are equally important. Only those of equal importance are separated with a comma. If you apply one or both of these tests, you can easily tell whether a comma is needed:

■ Change the order of the adjectives. If the sentence reads just as clearly, separate the adjectives with a comma. If the sentence becomes unclear or sounds awkward, do not use a comma. The first two example sentences make sense even if the position of the adjectives is changed. The last example sentence makes no sense if you change the order of any of the adjectives other than *intense* and *talented*. Therefore, those are the only adjectives separated by a comma.
  ✓ Alex avoided the **talkative, friendly, pleasant** boy sitting next to him at school.
  ✓ The carpenter repaired the floor with **aged, dark, oak** flooring.
  X The reporter spoke with **intense, several, high, talented, school** athletes.

■ A second, equally effective test is to place *and* between the adjectives. If the sentence still reads well, then use commas between the adjectives. If the sentence sounds unclear or awkward, do not use commas. Again, this works with the first two example sentences, but in the last sentence, *and* makes sense only between *intense* and *talented*. Where do commas go in the following sentences?

> We bought an **antique wrought iron** daybed.
> The envelope contained **three crisp clean brand-new** hundred dollar bills.

You should have punctuated the sentences like this:

> We bought an **antique, wrought iron** daybed.
> The envelope contained **three crisp, clean, brand-new** hundred dollar bills.

▶ Commas to Separate Other Elements of a Sentence

■ Use commas to separate contrasting or opposing elements in a sentence. The comma functions as a signal to the reader: What follows is an opposite idea. It makes the idea easier for the reader to grasp.
Examples:
> We searched the entire house**, but found nothing**.
> We need strong intellects, **not strong bodies,** to resolve this problem.
> The racers ran slowly at first**, quickly at the end**.
> We expected to meet the president, **not a White House aide**.

■ Use commas to separate words or phrases that interrupt the flow of thought in a sentence.
Examples:
> The deadline, **it seemed clear,** simply could not be met.
> We came to rely, **however,** on the kindness and generosity of the neighbors.
> The alternative route, **we discovered,** was faster than the original route.

■ Whenever the name of the person being addressed is included in a sentence, it should be set off by commas.
Examples:
> **Dave,** we wanted you to look at this layout before we sent it to printing.
> We wanted you to look at this layout, **Dave,** before we sent it to printing.
> We wanted you to look at this layout before we sent it to printing, **Dave**.

■ Mild exclamations included in a sentence are also set off with commas.
Examples:
> **Well,** that was certainly a pleasant surprise.
> **Yes,** I'll call you as soon as we get the information.
> **Heavens,** that was a long-winded speaker.

■ Use a comma after the greeting and closing of a letter.
Examples:
> Dear Uncle Jon,
> Sincerely,
> Yours truly,

Practice

Choose the correctly punctuated version of each of the following sets of sentences. Keep in mind what you learned about commas in the previous lesson.

14. a. Yes, I met with three prospective buyers, but I still want to meet a few more.
   b. Yes I met with three prospective buyers, but I still want to meet a few more.
   c. Yes, I met with three prospective buyers but I still want to meet a few more.

15. a. My daughter loved the museum, my son, on the other hand, was bored out of his mind.
   b. My daughter loved the museum; my son, on the other hand, was bored out of his mind.
   c. My daughter loved the museum, my son, on the other hand was bored out of his mind.

16. a. Well, Marcus, I hope that Lisa left you a number where she can be reached.
   b. Well, Marcus I hope that Lisa left you a number where she can be reached.
   c. Well Marcus, I hope that Lisa left you a number where she can be reached.

17. a. When I go to my yoga class, I need to bring comfortable clothes a yoga mat and a bottle of water.
   b. When I go to my yoga class I need to bring comfortable clothes, a yoga mat, and a bottle of water.
   c. When I go to my yoga class, I need to bring comfortable clothes, a yoga mat, and a bottle of water.

18. a. The restaurant I believe is located at 112 West Orange Street, Philadelphia, Pennsylvania.
   b. The restaurant, I believe, is located at 112 West Orange Street, Philadelphia, Pennsylvania.
   c. The restaurant, I believe, is located at 112, West Orange Street, Philadelphia, Pennsylvania.

19. a. Our newest employee, a transfer from the home office, is the strong silent absent type, I think.
   b. Our newest employee, a transfer from the home office is the strong, silent, absent type, I think.
   c. Our newest employee, a transfer from the home office, is the strong, silent, absent type, I think.

20. a. I'm afraid, Mr. Dobbs, that you lack the qualifications for this job; but we have another that might interest you.
   b. I'm afraid Mr. Dobbs, that you lack the qualifications for this job, but we have another that might interest you.
   c. I'm afraid, Mr. Dobbs, that you lack the qualifications for this job, but we have another that might interest you.

21. a. Usually, at the company picnic we play badminton, frisbee golf, volleyball, and horseshoes.
   b. Usually, at the company picnic, we play badminton frisbee golf, volleyball and horseshoes.
   c. Usually, at the company picnic, we play badminton, frisbee, golf, volleyball, and horseshoes.

22. a. We will advertise our biggest sale of the decade on June 21, 1997, the 25th anniversary of our Grand Opening sale.

b. We will advertise our biggest sale of the decade on June 21 1997, the 25th anniversary of our Grand Opening sale.

c. We will advertise our biggest sale of the decade on June 21, 1997 the 25th anniversary of our Grand Opening sale.

23. a. Exhausted by the heat, rather than the exertion, Ming collapsed under a tall shady oak tree.

b. Exhausted by the heat rather than the exertion, Ming collapsed under a tall, shady oak tree.

c. Exhausted by the heat, rather than the exertion, Ming collapsed under a tall, shady oak tree.

▶ Answers

1. You can safely view an eclipse through the viewing glass of a welding helmet, or you can look through a piece of overexposed film.

2. The prisoner showed no remorse as the guilty verdict was announced, nor did the tears of the victim's family arouse any emotion.

3. The young calf put its head over the fence, and it licked my hand.

4. Icebergs in the Antarctic are flat and smooth, but those in the Arctic are rough.

5. I understand your position on this issue; I still believe you are dead wrong.

6. I like Sam; he likes me, for we are best of friends.

7. The inventory is valued at one million dollars, but it's not enough to cover our debt.

8. If you know of anyone with data processing experience, encourage him or her to apply for this new position.

9. After he ran into the mayor's car with his truck, Adam used his cell phone to call the police, his doctor, lawyer, and insurance agent.

10. The homegrown philosopher, who lives next door at 251 Acorn Street, Libertyville, Kansas, claims to know exactly who invented the wheel, sliced bread, and kissing.

11. Estelle was born on January 31, 1953, and Arun was born on June 30, 1960.

12. Looking for a solution to the printing problem, Karissa asked an older employee, questioned the supervisor, and finally consulted the printer manual.

13. Baruch brought a jello salad to the potluck. Shannon brought peanuts, M&M's, mints, and pretzels.

14. a.

15. b.

16. a.

17. c.

18. b.

19. c.

20. c.

21. c.

22. a.

23. c.

Skill Building until Next Time

As you read the newspaper, a book, or written materials at work, take special note of the commas you see. Try to remember why a comma might be used in each of the situations. Since commas are one of the most frequently misused punctuation marks, look for places where other writers have misused them.

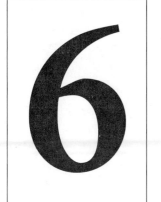

L E S S O N

6 ▶ Semicolons and Colons

LESSON SUMMARY

Many people are confused by semicolons (;) and colons (:), but after you work through this lesson, you'll know exactly what to do with both of them.

You learned to use semicolons to separate independent clauses in Lesson 3. In this lesson, you'll review that use of semicolons, as well as the use of some of the other punctuation marks you have studied so far. You will learn how to use semicolons with conjunctive adverbs and when to separate items in a series with semicolons. You will also learn to use colons in business communications and other settings.

Begin by seeing how much you know. Insert semicolons and colons where you think they are needed in the **Problem** column on the following page. Check yourself against the correct version in the **Solution** column on the right as you go.

Problem

Dear Mr. Powell

This letter is a formal complaint regarding service our company received from your representatives at 130 P.M. on January 26, 1996. These are the procedures for which we were billed a complete scotomy, a procedure to rid the machinery of electrostatic material a comprehensive assessment, a procedure for checking all mechanical and electronic parts in the machinery a thorough cleaning, a procedure necessary to keep the machine running efficiently.

This may be what the representative reported to have done however, only the first procedure in the list was finished. Only one of the three items was completed therefore, we should be refunded the amount charged for the other two services.

We are filing this complaint in accordance with your technical manual *McDounah New Age Electronics A Complete Manual*. This information is found in Volume 2, page 27 "Customers dissatisfied with our service for any reason have the right to file a full complaint within 10 (ten) days from the date of service. Such a complaint must be addressed in writing to Mr. Douglas Powell, Service Manager McDounah New Age Electronics Demming, Delaware. Mr. Powell will respond within two days to remedy the alleged problem or to refund the amount in question."

We appreciate your prompt attention to this matter.

Sincerely,

Solution

Dear Mr. Powell:

This letter is a formal complaint regarding service our company received from your representatives at 1:30 P.M. on January 26, 1996. These are the procedures for which we were billed: a complete scotomy, a procedure to rid the machinery of electrostatic material; a comprehensive assessment, a procedure for checking all mechanical and electronic parts in the machinery; a thorough cleaning, a procedure necessary to keep the machine running efficiently.

This may be what the representative reported to have done; however, only the first procedure in the list was finished. Only one of the three items was completed; therefore, we should be refunded the amount charged for the other two services.

We are filing this complaint in accordance with your technical manual *McDounah New Age Electronics: A Complete Manual.* This information is found in Volume 2, page 27: "Customers dissatisfied with our service for any reason have the right to file a full complaint within 10 (ten) days from the date of service. Such a complaint must be addressed in writing to Mr. Douglas Powell, Service Manager; McDounah New Age Electronics; Demming, Delaware. Mr. Powell will respond within two days to remedy the alleged problem or to refund the amount in question."

We appreciate your prompt attention to this matter.

Sincerely,

▶ Semicolons

There are three different cases in which a semicolon is used to separate independent clauses. (See Lesson 3 if you've forgotten what an independent clause is.)

- To separate independent clauses joined without a conjunction. This rule may seem familiar to you because it was also included in the last lesson.
  Examples:
  Three doctors began the research project; only one completed it.
  Discard the packaging; save the paperwork for accounting.
  The hour is over; it's time to stop working.

- To separate independent clauses that contain commas even if the clauses are joined by a conjunction. The semicolon helps the reader see where the break in thought occurs.

  Example:

  > The team needed new equipment, updated training manuals, and better professional advice; but since none of this was provided, they performed as poorly as they had in the previous competition.

- To separate independent clauses connected with a conjunctive adverb. Follow the adverb with a comma. A *conjunctive adverb* is an adverb that joins independent clauses. Conjunctive adverbs are punctuated differently than regular conjunctions. The first independent clause is followed by a semicolon; the conjunctive adverb is followed by a comma.

  Examples:

  > Our copy of the central warehouse catalog arrived after the budget deadline; **consequently,** our requests are late.

  > In the book *An American Childhood,* Annie Dillard recounts her experiences as a child; **furthermore,** she questions and speculates about the meaning of life.

Here is a complete list of words used as conjunctive adverbs.

accordingly	instead
besides	moreover
consequently	nevertheless
furthermore	otherwise
hence	therefore
however	thus

Many people confuse subordinating conjunctions, such as *because, though, until,* and *while,* with the conjunctive adverbs previously mentioned. The difference is important. A clause beginning with a subordinating conjunction is only a subordinate clause; it can't stand alone as a sentence. A clause with a conjunctive adverb is an *independent clause,* which should be separated from another independent clause with a period and capital letter or with a semicolon.

Here's a trick to determine whether the word that begins a clause is a conjunctive adverb. If you can move the word around within the clause, it's a conjunctive adverb. If you can't, it's probably a subordinating conjunction. For example, here are two main clauses:

> My paycheck was delayed. I couldn't pay my rent on time.

Here are two ways of joining those two main clauses:

> My paycheck was delayed; therefore, I couldn't pay my rent on time.
> I couldn't pay my rent on time because my paycheck was delayed.

Check whether the first version uses a conjunctive adverb. Can you move *therefore* around in its clause? Yes, you could say, "I couldn't, therefore, pay my rent on time." So *therefore* is a conjunctive adverb.

Use the same test to see whether *because* is a conjunctive adverb that should come after a semicolon. Can you move *because* around in its clause? "My paycheck because was delayed"? No. So *because* is a subordinating conjunction, and the clause it introduces is not a main clause.

There's one more way a semicolon is used to separate:

- Use a semicolon to separate items in a series if the items contain commas. Unlike items in a series separated by commas, a semicolon is used even when there IS a conjunction.

  Examples:

    The dates we are considering for our annual party are Thursday, **June 5; Saturday, June 7; Sunday, June 8; or** Monday, June 9.

    When we go to the lake, I am sure to take a pizza pan, a popcorn popper, and pancake **griddle; fishing** tackle, life jackets, and ski **equipment; and** puzzles, cards, board games, and my guitar.

    The expansion committee is considering locations in Columbus, **Ohio; Orange, California; Minton, Tennessee; and** Jacksonville, Florida.

Practice

Practice what you've learned by adding semicolons where they are needed in the following sentences. You will find the answers at the end of this lesson.

1. I need a break I've been working for five hours straight.

2. We have branch offices in Paris, France Berlin, Germany Stockholm, Sweden and Budapest, Hungary.

3. We had no problem meeting the deadline however, we were still able to find ways of streamlining production.

4. We ate Swiss steak, riced potatoes, steamed broccoli, and fresh bread for dinner but we still had room to eat apple pie for dessert.

5. Paige left some of the confidential documents sitting on her desk at work consequently, she worried about their safety all night long.

▶ Colons

Colons That Introduce

- Use a colon to introduce a list of items, as long as the part before the colon is already a complete sentence.

  Examples:

    These people were cast in the play: Andrea, Horatio, Thom, Alley, and Benito.

    We packed these items for the trip: cameras, dress clothes, scuba equipment, and beach wear.

- Do not use a colon if the list of items complements a verb; in other words, if it completes the meaning begun by the verb. Look at the previous sample sentences rewritten in such a way that a colon is not necessary.

  Examples:

    The people cast in the play were Kristin, Horatio, Thom, Alley, and Benito.

    For our trip, we packed cameras, dress clothes, scuba equipment, and beach wear.

- Use a colon to introduce a formal quotation.

  Example:

    John F. Kennedy ended the speech with these notable words: "Ask not what your country can do for you. Ask what you can do for your country."

- Use a colon to emphasize a word, phrase, or clause that adds particular emphasis to the main body of a sentence. Again, the part before the colon should already be a complete sentence.

  Example:

    The financial problems our company has been experiencing have been caused by one thing: poor planning.

    We were missing a vital piece of information: how the basic product design differed from last year's model.

Colons That Show a Subordinate Relationship

Use a colon to show a subordinate relationship in the following cases:

- Between two sentences when the second explains the first.

  Examples:

  Brenton shouted and threw his fists in the air: He had just set a new world record.

  Nicole put the check into her scrapbook rather than cashing it: It was the first check she had ever earned.

  Scott ignored the phone: He knew it was a salesman for whom he had no time.

- Between the title and the subtitle of a book.

  Examples:

  Internet Starter Kit: A Complete Guide to Cyberspace

  Beyond 2000: A Futuristic View of Time

  O Death, Where is Thy Sting: Tales from the Other Side

- Between volume and page number or between chapter and verse.

  Examples:

  World Book Encyclopedia V: 128

  New Age Journal of Medicine IX: 23

  John 3:16

  Genesis 1:1

  Psalms 23:2

- Between hour and minute.

  Examples:

  12:53 A.M.

  2:10 P.M.

- After the greeting of a business letter. You learned that commas are used after greetings in personal or friendly letters. A colon signals the reader that what is to follow is a business matter, something to be taken seriously. This is particularly true if you include the position, but not the name of the person to whom the letter is addressed. However, even in a business letter, the closing is followed by a comma.

  Examples:

  Dear Mr. Strange:

      Cordially,

  Dear Operations Manager:

      Respectfully submitted,

Practice

Choose the correctly punctuated version in each of the following sets of sentences. You will find the correct answers at the end of the lesson.

6. a. I found the vacation policy in the employee manual, Volume 1: 14.
  b. I found the vacation policy, in the employee manual, Volume 1: 14.
  c. I found the vacation policy in the employee manual Volume 1: 14

7. a. Margo said she completed the application, however the last two sections were still blank.
  b. Margo said she completed the application; however the last two sections were still blank.
  c. Margo said she completed the application; however, the last two sections were still blank.

8. a. When I go the employee retreat I'll need a tennis racket, a bathing suit, a pair of sneakers, and a towel.
  b. When I go the employee retreat, I'll need a tennis racket, a bathing suit, a pair of sneakers, and a towel.
  c. When I go the employee retreat, I'll need: a tennis racket, a bathing suit, a pair of sneakers, and a towel.

9. a. Dear Member,
The scheduled meeting will begin at 9,00 A.M. and will conclude before 10,30 A.M.

b. Dear Member:
The scheduled meeting will begin at 9:00 A.M. and will conclude before 10:30 A.M.

c. Dear Member;
The scheduled meeting will begin at 9:00 A.M. and will conclude before 10:30 A.M.

10. a. The movie will be shown on Tuesday at 2:00 P.M., 4:00 P.M., and 6:00 P.M.

b. The movie will be shown on Tuesday at 2:00 P.M.; 4:00 P.M., and 6:00 P.M.

c. The movie will be shown on Tuesday at 2:00, P.M.; 4:00, P.M.; and 6:00, P.M.

11. a. We agreed to plant tulips, a cheerful and colorful flower; daisies, a simply yet lovely crowd favorite; lavender, a delicate flowering herb; and ivy, a low-maintenance ground cover.

b. We agreed to plant tulips, a cheerful and colorful flower: daisies, a simply yet lovely crowd favorite: lavender, a delicate flowering herb: and ivy, a low-maintenance ground cover.

c. We agreed to plant tulips a cheerful and colorful flower, daisies a simply yet lovely crowd favorite, lavender a delicate flowering herb, and ivy, a low-maintenance ground cover.

12. a. The students learned the following information from the museum guide: the artist's name; the artist's date of birth; the artist's credentials; and the artist's general style.

b. The students learned the following information from the museum guide the artist's name, the artist's date of birth, the artist's credentials, and the artist's general style.

c. The students learned the following information from the museum guide: the artist's name, the artist's date of birth, the artist's credentials, and the artist's general style.

▶ Answers

1. I need a break; I've been working for five hours straight.

2. We have branch offices in Paris, France; Berlin, Germany; Stockholm, Sweden; and Budapest, Hungary.

3. We had no problem meeting the deadline; however, we were still able to find ways of streamlining production.

4. We ate Swiss steak, riced potatoes, steamed broccoli, and fresh bread for dinner; but we still had room to eat apple pie for dessert.

5. Paige left some of the confidential documents sitting on her desk at work; consequently, she worried about their safety all night long.

6. a.

7. c.

8. b.

9. b.

10. a.

11. a.

12. c.

Skill Building until Next Time

Take a look at some of the letters or communications you have received or written recently. Examine the punctuation. Did the author use endmarks, commas, semicolons, and colons correctly? If not, correct them. It will be good practice.

Apostrophes and Dashes

LESSON SUMMARY

This lesson will put you in control of apostrophes (') and dashes (—), two of the most commonly misused marks of punctuation.

Apostrophes communicate important information in written language. Dashes, when used sparingly, add emphasis. Before you begin the lesson, see how much you already know. Add apostrophes—and one pair of dashes—where you think they belong in the **Problem** column on the following page. Check yourself with the **Solution** column.

Problem

Marjorie is studying contemporary American history, and she is most interested in the history of the 50s and 60s. Shes taken most of the classes offered by her colleges history department, and she only has one semester to go before she graduates. In order to get her degree, however, she has to write a thesis, and shes having a difficult time deciding on the topic. She met with her advisor one of the leading experts on the civil rights movement and she talked with him about the possibility of focusing on the Montgomery Bus Boycott that began in 55. She also met with the professor of her womens history class and came away from that meeting inspired to write about the womens movement. She thought that her history study group might help with her decision, but the members opinions were split. Two of them wanted her to write about civil rights and the other two urged her to pursue the womens movement. She finally decided that she should stop seeking outside advice since any additional feedback would only confuse her further.

Solution

Marjorie is studying contemporary American history, and she is most interested in the history of the '50s and '60s. She's taken most of the classes offered by her college's history department, and she only has one semester to go before she graduates. In order to get her degree, however, she has to write a thesis, and she's having a difficult time deciding on the topic. She met with her advisor—one of the leading experts on the civil rights movement—and she talked with him about the possibility of focusing on the Montgomery Bus Boycott that began in '55. She also met with the professor of her women's history class and came away from that meeting inspired to write about the women's movement. She thought that her history study group might help with her decision, but the members' opinions were split. Two of them wanted her to write about civil rights and the other two urged her to pursue the women's movement. She finally decided that she should stop seeking outside advice, since any additional feedback would only confuse her further.

▶ Apostrophes

To Show Possession

Use an apostrophe to show possession. The highlighted words in each of the following examples are *possessive adjectives*: They show to whom or what a noun belongs.

SINGULAR NOUNS (ADD 'S)	PLURAL NOUNS ENDING IN S (ADD ')	PLURAL NOUNS NOT ENDING IN S
boy's toy (The toy is the **boy's**.)	**boys'** bicycles (The bicycles are the **boys'**.)	**men's** schedules (The schedules are the **men's**.)
child's play	**kids'** bedrooms	**children's** opinions
lady's coat	**ladies'** skirts	**women's** department
dentist's aide	**players'** representative	**people's** choice

Apostrophes are *not* used to form plurals. When you're thinking of putting an apostrophe in a noun that ends in *s*, ask yourself whether you're merely showing that there's more than one thing. If so, there's no apostrophe.

Examples:

There are a lot of **potatoes** in the refrigerator.
Cut out the **potatoes'** eyes.

You can avoid putting apostrophes in words that are merely plurals by trying this formula: *The _____ of the _____*, as in *the eyes of the potatoes.* If the words don't fit in that formula, the noun doesn't take an apostrophe.

Here are some special cases for the use of apostrophes to show possession.

- When there is more than one word in the possessive adjective—for example, with a compound noun, a business or institution, or jointly possessed items—add the apostrophe *s* to the last word of the compound.
  Examples:
  someone **else's** problem
  mother-in-**law's** visit
  board of **directors'** policy
  Pope John Paul **II's** death
  Proctor and **Gamble's** product
  Wayne and **Judy's** log cabin
- Words showing periods of time or amounts of money need apostrophes when used as possessive adjectives.
  Examples:
  day's pay, **month's** vacation, **morning's** work
  two **cents'** worth, **dollar's** worth
- A singular noun that ends in *s* still takes apostrophe *s*, though some writers omit the *s* and include only the apostrophe.
  Examples:
  Roger **Maris's** batting record
  Lotus's personal organizer

- When a possessive pronoun (*my, mine, our, ours, your, yours, his, her, hers, their, theirs*) is used as an adjective, no apostrophe is needed.
  Examples:
  This is **their** idea. The idea is **theirs.**
  We filed **our** flight plan. The flight plan is **ours.**
  This manual must be **yours.**

Practice

From each set that follows, choose the option in which apostrophes are used correctly. You will find the answers to each set of questions at the end of the lesson.

1. a. An employee's motivation is different from an owner's.
   b. An employees' motivation is different from an owners'.

2. a. Employees reward's differ from an owners'.
   b. Employees' rewards differ from an owner's.

3. a. Elaine has worked three years as a physicians assistant.
   b. Elaine has worked three years as a physician's assistant.

4. a. The Mens' Issue's group meets every Saturday morning.
   b. The Men's Issues group meets every Saturday morning.

5. a. The companies' sales force has doubled in recent years, and the credit is your's.
   b. The company's sales force has doubled in recent years, and the credit is yours.

6. a. The most efficient method is her's.
   b. The most efficient method is hers.

7. a. After five years' experience, we earn four weeks' paid vacation.

   b. After five year's experience, we earn four week's paid vacation.

8. a. Pat and Janice's proposal requires a month's work.

   b. Pat's and Janice's proposal requires a months' work.

9. a. The computer supply store's top-selling printer is Hewlett Packards latest model.

   b. The computer supply store's top-selling printer is Hewlett Packard's latest model.

10. a. Ms. Jones's boutique sells the same products as Mr. Smith's.

   b. Ms. Jones boutique sells the same products as Mr. Smiths.

To Show Omission

Use an apostrophe to show that letters or numbers have been omitted.

   Examples:

   Morton **doesn't** (does not) live here anymore.

   The officer **couldn't** (could not) give me a speeding ticket.

   Who's (who is) on first?

   I just **can't** (cannot) understand this memo.

   My first car was a **'67** (1967) Chevy.

   Grandpa tells stories about life in the **'40s** (1940s).

▶ Dashes

A *dash* is a very specialized punctuation mark reserved for only a few special situations. However, many writers use it incorrectly in place of other marks. Dashes call attention to themselves. A careful writer uses them sparingly. Dashes are very effective if used correctly, but they lose their impact if overused.

Remember to distinguish a dash from a hyphen when typing. A dash is **two** hyphens.

- Use a dash to mark a sudden break in thought or to insert a comment.
  Examples:

   Here is your sandwich and your—Look out for that bee!

   I remember the day—what middle-aged person doesn't—that President Kennedy was shot.

   John is sorry—we all are—about your unfortunate accident.

- Use a dash to emphasize explanatory material. You don't have to use a dash, but you may.
  Examples:

   Knowing yourself—your thoughts, values, and dreams—is the most important knowledge.

   "The writer is by nature a dreamer—a conscious dreamer." —*Carson McCullers*

   We spend our summers in Canada—Ontario, to be precise.

- Use a dash to indicate omitted letters or words.
  Examples:

   "Oh, da—, I can't believe I forgot to mail that package!"

   "Hello?—Yes, I can hear you just fine.—Of course—I think I can.—Good!—I'll see you later.—"

- Use a dash to connect a beginning phrase to the rest of the sentence.
  Examples:

   Honesty, integrity, tenacity—these are marks of motivated salespeople.

   Nashville, Tennesse; Olympia, Washington; Oceola, Iowa—these are the prospective locations.

Practice

Choose the option in which dashes and other punctuation are used correctly in each of the following sets.

11. a. The instructor had only one goal—to be sure everyone learned the basics of web design.
   b. The instructor had only one goal to be sure everyone learned—the basics of web design.

12. a. Her preference—just in case anyone asks, is to find an inexpensive Italian restaurant for dinner.
   b. Her preference—just in case anyone asks— is to find an inexpensive Italian restaurant for dinner.

13. a. Mr. Jackson can be such an annoying, I suppose I should be careful about what I say.
   b. Mr. Jackson can be such an annoying—I suppose I should be careful about what I say.

14. a. New York, Chicago, Atlanta—these are the cities on her itinerary.
   b. New York, Chicago, Atlanta: These are the cities on her itinerary.

15. a. I've managed to misplace that d— memo that I wrote—Oh, it's right on my desk.
   b. I've managed to misplace that d— memo that I wrote, Oh it's right on my desk.

► Practice and Review

Check yourself with these sample test questions. These extremely difficult questions cover much of what you have learned about punctuation so far. Look at the items carefully. Which of the following options is punctuated correctly?

16. a. Although it may seem strange, my partners purpose in interviewing Dr. E.S. Sanders Jr., was to eliminate him as a suspect in the crime.
   b. Although it may seem strange my partner's purpose in interviewing Dr. E.S. Sanders, Jr. was to eliminate him, as a suspect in the crime.
   c. Although it may seem strange, my partner's purpose in interviewing Dr. E.S. Sanders, Jr., was to eliminate him as a suspect in the crime.
   d. Although it may seem strange, my partner's purpose in interviewing Dr. E.S. Sanders, Jr. was to eliminate him, as a suspect in the crime.

17. a. After colliding with a vehicle at the intersection of Grand, and Forest Ms. Anderson saw a dark hooded figure reach through the window, grab a small parcel and run north on Forest.
   b. After colliding with a vehicle at the intersection of Grand, and Forest, Ms. Anderson saw a dark hooded figure reach through the window, grab a small parcel, and run north on Forest.
   c. After colliding with a vehicle at the intersection of Grand and Forest Ms. Anderson saw a dark, hooded figure reach through the window, grab a small parcel and run north on Forest.
   d. After colliding with a vehicle at the intersection of Grand and Forest, Ms. Anderson saw a dark, hooded figure reach through the window, grab a small parcel, and run north on Forest.

18.

    a. When we interviewed each of the boys and the fathers, we determined that the men's stories did not match up with the boy's versions.

    b. When we interviewed each of the boys and the fathers, we determined that the men's stories did not match up with the boys' versions.

    c. When we interviewed each of the boys and the fathers, we determined that the mens' stories did not match up with the boys' versions.

    d. When we interviewed each of the boy's and the father's, we determined that the men's stories did not match up with the boys' versions.

19.

    a. Bring these items when you drive up here tomorrow—Bobbys sleeping bag, another can of insect repellent, the girls queen-sized air mattress—they want to use it to sunbathe on the water, and my swimming trunks.

    b. Bring these items when you drive up here tomorrow: Bobby's sleeping bag, another can of insect repellent, the girls' queen-sized air mattress—they want to use it to sunbathe on the water—and my swimming trunks.

    c. Bring these items when you drive up here tomorrow: Bobby's sleeping bag, another can of insect repellent, the girl's queen-sized air mattress—they want to use it to sunbathe on the water, and my swimming trunks.

    d. Bring these items when you drive up here tomorrow. Bobby's sleeping bag, another can of insect repellent, the girls queen-sized air mattress, they want to use it to sunbathe on the water, and my swimming trunks.

20.

    a. James Autry, Stephen Covey, Madeline Hunter—these authors are responsible for my management style, a combination of Autry's personnel philosophy, Covey's process for prioritizing, and Hunter's organizational principles.

    b. James Autry, Stephen Covey, Madeline Hunter. These authors are responsible for my management style, a combination of Autry's personnel philosophy, Covey's process for prioritizing and Hunter's organizational principles.

    c. James Autry, Stephen Covey, Madeline Hunter—these authors are responsible for my management style, a combination of Autrys personnel philosophy, Coveys process for prioritizing and Hunters organizational principles.

    d. James Autry, Stephen Covey, Madeline Hunter: These authors are responsible for my management style; a combination of Autry's personnel philosophy; Covey's process for prioritizing; and Hunter's organizational principles.

▶ Answers

1. a.	**11.** a.
2. b.	**12.** b.
3. b.	**13.** b.
4. b.	**14.** a.
5. b.	**15.** a.
6. b.	**16.** c.
7. a.	**17.** d.
8. a.	**18.** b.
9. b.	**19.** b.
10. a.	**20.** a.

Skill Building until Next Time

Few people understand the rules of apostrophes and dashes fully. Advertisers are notorious for misusing both types of punctuation. Pay special attention to billboards and advertisements in newspapers and magazines. Look for places where apostrophes and dashes are used correctly. Notice places where they are omitted or added when they shouldn't be. If your job produces promotional material, examine some of your own literature to see if apostrophes and dashes have been used correctly.

Quotation Marks

LESSON SUMMARY

This lesson covers rules regarding the use of quotation marks, both double and single. Although these marks are most often found in dialogue, they are important in other writing situations as well.

egin this lesson by seeing how much you already know about quotation marks. Insert them where you think they belong in the sentences in the **Problem** column on the following page. Some sentences will also need endmarks and commas. Check yourself against the corrected versions of the sentences in the **Solution** column.

PROBLEM	SOLUTION
The essay that won the prize was called The Entrepreneurial Life.	The essay that won the prize was called "The Entrepreneurial Life."
Marty loved seafood, but he hadn't heard of tilapia before coming to this restaurant.	Marty loved seafood, but he hadn't heard of "tilapia" before coming to this restaurant.
Out of the water! shouted the lifeguard.	"Out of the water!" shouted the lifeguard.
She's been late three times this—Carlos stopped abruptly as Lydia walked by his desk.	"She's been late three times this—" Carlos stopped abruptly as Lydia walked by his desk.
The motivational speaker used the word visualize ten times during his speech.	The motivational speaker used the word "visualize" ten times during his speech.
The lead article is titled Mutual Funds at a Glance.	The lead article is titled "Mutual Funds at a Glance."
If she's not here in fifteen minutes, said Eileen, we'll have to leave without her.	"If she's not here in fifteen minutes," said Eileen, "we'll have to leave without her."
Where are the other members of the focus group? the marketing manager asked. They were supposed to be here an hour ago.	"Where are the other members of the focus group?" the marketing manager asked. "They were supposed to be here an hour ago."
Georgia is aptly nicknamed the Peach State.	Georgia is aptly nicknamed the "Peach State."
With her gloomy disposition, I can see why you call her Jolly Janice.	With her gloomy disposition, I can see why you call her "Jolly Janice."
Our bonus for working during the holiday weekend was a box of donuts.	Our "bonus" for working during the holiday weekend was a box of donuts.
The poem she decided to read at the ceremony was The Daffodils by William Wordsworth.	The poem she decided to read at the ceremony was "The Daffodils" by William Wordsworth.
Nell said, The clerk yelled, Go away! before she had a chance to tell her why she was there.	Nell said, "The clerk yelled, 'Go away!' before she had a chance to tell her why she was there."

► Quotation Marks with Direct Quotations

- Use quotation marks to set off a direct quotation or thought within a sentence or paragraph. This includes quotations that are signed, etched, inscribed, carved, and so on.

Examples:
  Mr. Hurley called our prototype "a model of pure genius."
  I was certain he said, "Campbells will accept delivery on Tuesday."
  "When will help arrive?" I wondered.
  The sign clearly read, "No trespassing."
  "Happy and Fulfilled," the headstone read.

- Do *not* use quotation marks for paraphrases or indirect quotations.

   Examples:

   > I was sure Campbells wanted a Tuesday delivery. I wondered when help would arrive.

   > The sign said that trespassing and hunting were not allowed.

- Use single quotation marks to set off a quotation within a quotation.

   Examples:

   > "I distinctly heard her say, 'The store opens at 9:00,'" said Gene.

   > The speaker continued, "I am ever mindful of Franklin Roosevelt's famous words, 'We have nothing to fear but fear itself.' But fear is a terrible thing."

   > My speech teacher asked, "Does anyone in this room remember the way Jim Nabors used to say, 'Golly'?"

A Word about Dialogue

Correctly punctuating dialogue means understanding how to use quotation marks, commas, and endmarks. Take a close look at the sentences in the following dialogue sample. They include the basic dialogue structures. The words quoted are called *quotations*, and the words explaining who said the quotations are called *tags*. In this sample, the tags are highlighted.

1. "I'm really thirsty. Let's grab something to drink," **said Horace.**
2. **Nancy replied,** "I'm thirsty, but I don't have any cash. Do you have some?"
3. "I don't get it," **Horace answered.** "You're the manager with the high-paying job."
4. "Well," **Nancy replied,** "credit cards are all I ever use."

Quoted words are always surrounded by quotation marks. Place quotation marks before a group of quoted words and again at the end.

Tags are punctuated differently depending upon where they appear in the sentence. Whenever the tag follows a quotation and the quotation is a sentence that would normally be punctuated with a period, use a comma at the end of the quotation. The period comes at the end of the tag. However, if the quotation is a sentence that would normally be followed with a question mark or an exclamation point, insert the question mark or exclamation point at the end of the quotation. Place a period after the tag. (See sentence 1 in the previous column.)

> "I'm really thirsty. Let's grab something to drink," said Alvina.

> "I'm really thirsty. Do you want to grab something to drink?" asked Alvina.

> "I'm really thirsty. Hold it—a Dairy Queen!" exclaimed Alvina.

Sometimes, the tag precedes the quotation. When this happens, place a comma after the tag. Put quotation marks around the quoted words, capitalize the first word of the quotation, and punctuate the sentence as you would normally. (See sentence 2.)

Sometimes, the tag interrupts the quotation. If both the first and second parts of the quotation are complete sentences, the first part of the quotation is punctuated in the same way as a quotation with the tag at the end. In other words, the period follows the tag. The rest of the quotation is punctuated in the same way as a quotation preceded by a tag. (See sentence 3.)

When the tag interrupts the quotation and the sentence, the words preceding the tag begin the thought, and the words following the tag complete the thought. Place quotation marks around the quoted words and follow the first part of the quotation with a comma. Place a comma after the tag (not a period, since the sentence is not completed). Place quotation marks around the last part of the quotation, but **do not** capitalize the first letter of the quotation. It is not the beginning of a sentence. Punctuate the rest of the sentence as you would normally. (See sentence 4.)

NOTE: All the punctuation is **inside** the quotation marks except the punctuation marks following the tags.

Dialogue at a Glance

- Tag following the quotation mark:
  "_____," said Rose.
  "_____?" asked Rose.
  "_____!" exclaimed Rose.

- Tag preceding quotation:
  Iris said, "_____."
  Iris asked, "_____?"
  Iris exclaimed, "_____!"

- Tag between two sentences of a quotation:
  "_____," said Lily. "_____."
  "_____?" asked Lily. "_____?"
  "_____!" exclaimed Lily. "_____!"

- Tag interrupting a quotation and a sentence:
  "_____," said Daisy, "_____."
  "_____," asked Daisy, "_____?"
  "_____," exclaimed Daisy, "_____!"

▶ Other Uses of Quotation Marks

- Use quotation marks to set off unfamiliar terms and nicknames. You will often see italics used in the same manner.
  Examples:
  None of us had heard of "chutney" before we read the article.
  He was dubbed "Sir Tagalong" by the other members of the staff.
  The Scrabble players disagreed over the term "ptu." (or . . . over the term *ptu.*)

- Use quotation marks to indicate irony or raised eyebrows. But avoid overusing quotation marks in this way; it doesn't work if you do it all the time.
  Examples:
  When we were camping, our "bathroom" was a thicket behind our tent.
  Our "guide" never mentioned the presence of poison ivy.
  The "fun" of surgery begins long before the operation commences.

- Use quotation marks to set off titles of certain items. Other titles should be underlined or italicized.

ENCLOSE IN QUOTATION MARKS	UNDERLINE OR ITALICIZE
name of a short story or chapter of a book	title of a novel
name of a TV program	name of a movie
title of a poem	title of a collection of poetry or an epic poem
headline of an article or title of a report	name of a magazine or newspaper
title of a song	title of a musical, play, or long musical composition
	name of a ship, plane, train, etc.

▶ Punctuating within Quotation Marks

Here are the rules regarding the use of other punctuation marks and quotation marks.

- Question marks, exclamation points, and dashes go inside the quotation marks if they are part of the quotation. If they are not, place them outside the quotation marks.
  Examples:
    The doctor asked, "Can you feel any pain in this area?" [Part of the quotation]
    Have you read Nathaniel Hawthorne's "The Birthmark"? [Not part of the quotation]
    "I wish I'd never heard of—" Karen stopped abruptly as Nick walked in the room. [Part of the quotation]
    "Stage left," "stage right," "upstage," and "downstage"—I always confused these terms. [Not part of the quotation]
- Periods and commas go **inside** closing quotation marks.
    "Let's wait a few minutes," suggested Doris, "before we leave."
- Colons and semicolons go **outside** closing quotation marks.
    I can see only one challenge for the speaker of "The Road Less Traveled": ambivalence.
    The critic called the latest sculpture an "abomination to sensitive eyes"; the artist was hurt.

Practice

Choose the correctly punctuated version in each of the following sets of sentences. Also, check for punctuation other than quotation marks.

1. a. "Have you ever read the story 'The Open Window' by O. Henry? asked Martha.
   b. "Have you ever read the story 'The Open Window' by O. Henry?" asked Martha.
   c. "Have you ever read the story "The Open Window" by O. Henry?" asked Martha.

2. a. Did you know it was Winston Churchill who called Russia "a riddle wrapped up in a mystery inside an enigma"?
   b. Did you know it was "Winston Churchill" who called Russia "a riddle wrapped up in a mystery inside an enigma?"
   c. Did you know it was Winston Churchill who called Russia "a riddle wrapped up in a mystery inside an enigma?"

3. a. After reading a review of Toy Story, I wanted to see the movie.
   b. After reading a review of <u>Toy Story</u>, I wanted to see the movie.
   c. After reading a review of "Toy Story," I wanted to see the movie.

4. a. Leaving five minutes early on Friday was our "reward."
   b. Leaving five minutes early on Friday was our "reward".
   c. Leaving five minutes early on Friday was our 'reward.'

5. a. "Firewall," "bandwidth," "URL"—these are some of the technical terms you'll learn in this class.
   b. "Firewall," "bandwidth," "URL—" these are some of the technical terms you'll learn in this class.
   c. "Firewall", "bandwidth", "URL"—these are some of the technical terms you'll learn in this class.

6. a. If you read my article Budget Play in this morning's *Register,* you'll understand why I'm so cynical about Washington politicians.

b. If you read my article "Budget Play" in this morning's "Register", you'll understand why I'm so cynical about Washington politicians.

c. If you read my article "Budget Play" in this morning's *Register*, you'll understand why I'm so cynical about Washington politicians.

7. a. "The story 'What Does Anyone Really Understand?' certainly gave me something to think about," remarked Uncle Art.

b. 'The story "What Does Anyone Really Understand?" certainly gave me something to think about,' remarked Uncle Art.

c. "The story "What Does Anyone Really Understand?" certainly gave me something to think about," remarked Uncle Art.

8. a. "Do you name all your cats Howard," asked my friend Ted.

b. "Do you name all your cats Howard"? asked my friend Ted.

c. "Do you name all your cats Howard?" asked my friend Ted.

9. a. The officer asked us whether we had seen the accident.

b. The officer asked us whether we had seen the accident?

c. The officer asked us, "Whether we had seen the accident."

10. a. "You would be better off not to offer any excuses," the personnel director advised, "I'm afraid that will only make matters worse."

b. "You would be better off not to offer any excuses." the personnel director advised. "I'm afraid that will only make matters worse."

c. "You would be better off not to offer any excuses," the personnel director advised. "I'm afraid that will only make matters worse."

▶ **Answers**

1. b.
2. a.
3. b.
4. a.
5. a.
6. c.
7. a.
8. c.
9. a.
10. c.

Skill Building until Next Time

Look for examples of quotation marks in anything you read. When you find them, check to see if they've been used correctly.

"Designer" Punctuation

LESSON SUMMARY

This lesson covers some of the less commonly used punctuation marks, including hyphens, parentheses, brackets, ellipses, and diagonal slashes. While these marks aren't necessary all that often, when they *are* necessary, it's important to use them correctly.

The punctuation marks covered in this lesson—hyphens, parentheses, brackets, ellipses, and diagonals—are not often used in regular writing. However, they serve very specific purposes. Knowing and understanding their functions gives a writer an advantage in communicating ideas. Since most of these rules are so specialized that only a few people know them, we'll begin immediately with the lesson rather than with an assessment of your current knowledge. The last part of the lesson discusses using numbers in written text.

▶ Hyphens

The main purpose of a hyphen (-) is to join words in creating compound nouns or adjectives. Hyphens signal words that work together for a single purpose.

Compound nouns may be written as a single word, as two words, or as a hyphenated word. Whenever you are in doubt, consult a recent dictionary. Since language changes constantly, these words also evolve. A compound noun written as two words may come to be written as a hyphenated word and eventually become a single word.

For example, the word *semicolon* began as two separate words: *semi colon*. In the late 1950s, dictionaries began listing it as a hyphenated word: *semi-colon*. A recent dictionary will list it as a single word: *semicolon*.

SINGLE-WORD COMPOUND NOUNS	TWO-WORD COMPOUND NOUNS	HYPHENATED COMPOUND NOUNS
tablecloth	parking lot	jack-in-the-box
horsefly	couch potato	brother-in-law
textbook	floppy disk	money-maker
catwalk		city-state
bedroom		well-being
		merry-go-round

- Use a hyphen to join two coequal nouns working together as one.

  Shannon is a **teacher-poet.**

  Pete Rose was a **player-coach** for the Cincinnati Reds.

  Kevin Costner has joined the ranks of well-known **actor-directors**.

- Use a hyphen to join multi-word compound nouns.

  fly-by-night, stick-in-the-mud, good-for-nothing, three-year-old

- Use a hyphen to join two or more words that function as a single adjective *preceding* the noun.

  The hikers saw a **run-down** cabin in the clearing.

  Much has been written about the **Kennedy-Nixon** debates.

  An **ill-trained** police officer is more of a menace than protector.

  The company employed a **high-powered** consultant.

  A **soft-spoken** answer to the angry accusation ended the disagreement.

  His **off-the-wall** remarks keep our meetings lively and interesting.

  The parties finally agreed after three months of **hard-nosed** negotiations.

  A **French-Canadian** bicyclist won the **three-week** race.

- If the words functioning as a single adjective *follow* the noun, they are not hyphenated.

  The cabin the hikers saw in the clearing was **run down.**

  A police officer who is **ill trained** is more of a menace than a protector.

  The consultant employed by the company was **high powered**.

  The parties finally agreed after three months of negotiations that were **hard nosed**.

- Use a hyphen to join prefixes such as *self, half, ex, all, great, post, pro,* and *vice,* or the suffix *elect,* to words.*

  Harry Truman unleashed the **all-powerful** atomic weapon.

  Abraham Lincoln was a **self-made** man.

  Keep your **half-baked** ideas to yourself.

  Simone spotted her **ex-husband** walking into the grocery store.

  My **great-grandfather** turns 102 next Wednesday.

  Many remember the **post-WWII** years with great fondness.

  The **secretary-elect** picked up all the records from the presiding secretary.

---

* Refer to a dictionary for common words to determine if they still use the hyphen or if they are closed up.

Conservatives consider the front-runner to be a **proabortion** candidate. (per Merriam-Webster)

You are almost **halfway** through this book. (per Merriam-Webster)

- Use a hyphen to avoid confusion or awkward spellings.

    The coach decided to **re-pair** [rather than repair] the debate partners.

    The neighbors decided to **re-cover** [rather than recover] their old sofa.

    The sculpture had a **bell-like** [rather than belllike] shape.

- Use a hyphen to join a capital letter to a word.

    The **U-joint** went out in our second car.

    The architect worked with nothing more than a **T-square**.

- Use a hyphen to write two-word numbers between 21 and 99 as words.

    twenty-six, thirty-three, sixty-four, seventy-two, ninety-nine

- Use a hyphen to join fractions written as words.

    three-fifths, five-sixteenths, five thirty-seconds

- Use a hyphen to join numbers to words used as a single adjective.

    three-yard pass, eight-inch steel, two-word sentence, five-stroke lead

NOTE: When a series of similar number-word adjectives is written in a sentence, use a hyphen/comma combination with all but the last item in the series.

    Precut particle board comes in **two-, four-,** and **six-foot** squares.

    Andy scored three touchdowns on **eight-, fourteen-,** and **two-yard** runs.

- Use a hyphen to join numbers and adjectives.

    fifty-four-year-old woman, ten-dollar profit, two-thousand-acre ranch, twenty-minute wait

- Use a hyphen to write the time of day as words.

    twelve-thirty, four-o'clock appointment, six-fifteen A.M., one-fifty-five in the morning

- Use a hyphen to join numbers indicating a life span, a score, or the duration of an event.

    Abraham Lincoln (**1809-1865**) served as the sixteenth President, **1861-1865**.

    The Cowboys beat the Eagles **21-3**.

- Use a hyphen to separate a word between syllables at the end of a line. Here are a few guidelines for dividing words:

    - Never leave a single-letter syllable on a line.
    - Divide hyphenated words at the hyphen.
    - Never divide a one-syllable word.
    - Avoid dividing words that have fewer than six letters.
    - Avoid dividing the last word of a paragraph.
    - Avoid dividing a number.
    - Always check a dictionary if you are in doubt.

▶ Parentheses

- Use parentheses to enclose explanatory material that interrupts the normal flow of the sentences and is only marginally related to the text.

    Thirty-sixth Street (a party street if there ever was one) is a fun place to live.

    Our neighbors threw a huge party on New Year's Eve. (Fortunately, we were invited.)

    Unfortunately, another set of neighbors (who was not invited) called the police to complain about the noise.

    We party-goers (how were we to know?) were completely surprised by the officers.

Notice the last three sentences. Each set of parentheses contains a complete sentence. If the parenthetical construction comes at the end of a sentence, it is punctuated as its own sentence within the parentheses. On the other hand, if it comes within another sentence, no capital letters or periods are necessary. However, if the parenthetical construction in the middle of another sentence is a sentence that would normally require a question mark or exclamation point, include that punctuation.

- Use parentheses to enclose information when accuracy is essential.

    The two sons of Richard Hannika (Scott and William) are sole heirs to his fortune.

    We hereby agree to sell the heirloom for sixty-three dollars ($63.00).

- Use parentheses to enclose letters or numbers marking a division.

    This lesson includes several little-used, often-misused punctuation marks: (a) hyphens, (b) parentheses, (c) brackets, (d) diagonals, and (e) ellipses.

    Your task consists of three steps: (1) locating information, (2) writing a report, and (3) delivering a presentation about your findings.

▶ Brackets

- Use brackets to enclose parenthetical material within parentheses.

    Brandi planned to work as an aeronautic engineer (she completed an internship at National Aeronautics and Space Administration [NASA]) as soon as she completed her doctoral work.

- Use brackets to enclose words inserted into a quotation.

    "The next head nurse [Shawna DeWitt] will face the challenge of operating the floor with a reduced staff."

- Use brackets around the word *sic* to show that an error in a quotation was made by the original writer or speaker.

    "Unless we heel [sic] the nation's economic woes, social problems will continue to mount."

▶ Ellipses

Points of ellipsis look like periods, but they do not function as endmarks. Type three periods to form ellipses. These marks indicate omitted material or long pauses.

- Use ellipses to show that quoted material has been omitted. If the omission comes at the end of a sentence, follow the ellipses with a period.

    "Four-score and seven years ago . . . equal."

    "We hold these truths to be self-evident. . . ."

- Use ellipses to indicate a pause or hesitation.

    And the winner for "Best Actor" is . . . Dustin Hoffman.

    I think that adds up to . . . exactly eighty-three dollars.

▶ Diagonals

Much like the hyphen, a diagonal is a mark used to join words or numbers. The most frequent use of the diagonal is with the phrase *and/or*, which shows that the sentence refers to one or both of the words being joined.

    For breakfast, we can make bacon and/or French toast.

    Vinegar and/or egg whites added to plain water will make an excellent hair rinse that leaves hair soft and silky.

- Use a diagonal to separate numbers in a fraction.

    Normally, it takes us 3½ hours to sort the bulk mail at the end of the week.

    You'll need a 1⅝-inch wrench for this nut.

- Use a diagonal to show line divisions in poetry.

    "Goodnight, goodnight, parting is such sweet sorrow / That I shall say good night 'till it be morrow. / Sleep dwell upon thine eyes and peace in thy breast! / Would I were sleep and peace so sweet to rest!"

- Use a diagonal to indicate *per* or *divided by*.

    The cars in the new fleet average over 25 miles/gallon.

    Shares are calculated in this way: net profit/number of shareholders.

▶ Numbers

A few rules guide the use of numbers in writing. In journalistic writing, numbers are preferable to words because they are easier to identify and read. However, a number at the beginning of a sentence is always written as a word. In more formal writing, follow the conventions listed below.

- Use Arabic rather than Roman numerals: *1, 2, 3, 4* rather than *I, II, III, IV.*
- If a number can be written as one or two words, write it as a word. Otherwise, write the numeral: 8, twenty-six, 124, three hundred, 8,549, five million.
- Always write a number at the beginning of sentence as a word even if it is more than two words.

Practice

Add hyphens where they are needed in the following sentences.

1. Ms. Lewis, now an ex teacher, was one of the most high powered realtors in town.

2. Dr. Pratt was so concerned about the two year old girl's injury that he ordered an X ray.

3. Judy's well written essay impressed all twenty five judges.

4. After the three hour meeting, the soft spoken facilitator had convinced every member that their year end investment would yield a fifty dollar profit.

5. Anne won the three hundred meter freestyle by twenty six hundredths of a second.

Add hyphens, parentheses, brackets, ellipses, and diagonals where they are needed in the following sentences.

6. Muhammad Ali one of the greatest boxers of our time wrote a poem describing himself as someone who could "…float like a butterflie sic, sting like a bee."

7. After the workshop, please 1 collect the completed forms 2 compile all the data and 3 leave your report in Mr. White's right hand drawer.

8. Prizes for the three week contest can be collected in the form of cash and or merchandise and approximately one third of our members will be eligible.

▶ Answers

1. Ms. Lewis, now an ex-teacher, was one of the most high-powered realtors in town.
2. Dr. Pratt was so concerned about the two-year-old girl's injury that he ordered an X-ray.
3. Judy's well-written essay impressed all twenty-five judges.
4. After the three-hour meeting, the soft-spoken facilitator had convinced every member that their year-end investment would yield a fifty-dollar profit.
5. Anne won the three-hundred-meter freestyle by twenty-six hundredths of a second.
6. Muhammad Ali (one of the greatest boxers of our time) wrote a poem describing himself as someone who could "…float like a butterflie [sic], sting like a bee."
7. After the workshop, please (1) collect the completed forms, (2) compile all the data, and (3) leave your report in Mr. White's right-hand drawer.
8. Prizes for the three-week contest can be collected in the form of cash and/or merchandise and approximately one-third of our members will be eligible.

Skill Building until Next Time

Look for examples of the punctuation marks from this lesson as you read today. Since they are used less frequently than other marks, you probably won't see them as often. When you do, try to remember how the mark is used. Be especially aware of hyphens, parentheses, brackets, diagonals, and ellipses in advertising copy; check to see if they have been used correctly.

10 ▶ Verb Tense

LESSON SUMMARY

Verbs—words for actions or states of being—are what drive written language and give it life. Because verbs are so important, mistakes involving verbs really stand out. Those mistakes are also often tested on exams. This lesson and the next two will help you avoid some of the most common errors with verbs.

Writers use words to establish their credibility. Few things cast doubt on a writer's believability as much as misusing words—especially verbs. Incorrect verb forms call special attention to themselves and bring the writer's education and intelligence into question. Furthermore, exams often test your knowledge of how to use verbs and avoid errors involving verbs.

This lesson explains how to use verbs correctly and highlights a few of the most common mistakes writers make. See how many of the seven errors in verb usage you can find in the **Problem** version of the passage on the following page. In the **Solution** column, the paragraph is rewritten with the correct verb forms. As you go through the lesson, try to apply the rules you learn to these corrections.

Problem

Wendy circles five advertisements in last Sunday's newspaper. She had been looking for a job for three months and she is starting to get nervous about finding one. The money her mother had gave her was starting to run out and she knows she couldn't asked for more. If she was more qualified, she would of received a job offer already. However, she had very little work experience and the job market was particularly competitive at this time of year. As she start to write cover letters for this week's jobs, she wondered if she should met with a career counselor for advice.

Solution

Wendy circled five advertisements in last Sunday's newspaper. She had been looking for a job for three months and she was starting to get nervous about finding one. The money her mother had given her was starting to run out and she knew she couldn't ask for more. If she were more qualified, she would have received a job offer already. However, she had very little work experience and the job market was particularly competitive at this time of year. As she started to write cover letters for this week's jobs, she wondered if she should meet with a career counselor for advice.

▶ Principal Parts of Verbs

Verbs have three principal parts:

- **Present**—the form of the verb that would complete the sentence, "Today, I _____."
- **Past**—the form of the verb that would complete the sentence, "Yesterday, I _____."
- **Past participle**—the form of the verb that would complete the sentence, "Often, I have _____."

For most verbs, it's easy to form the three principal parts if you know the present form. Take the verb *look*, for example. *Today, I look. Yesterday, I looked. Often, I have looked.* For regular verbs, the past and past participle forms both add *–ed* to the present form. But English is full of irregular verbs that form the past and past participle in some other way. The following table shows the principal parts of several often misused verbs.

THREE PRINCIPAL PARTS OF VERBS		
PRESENT	**PAST**	**PAST PARTICIPLE***
do	did	done
go	went	gone
see	saw	seen
drink	drank	drunk
break	broke	broken
bring	brought	brought
choose	chose	chosen
know	knew	known
wear	wore	worn
write	wrote	written

* **Note:** Past participles must be preceded by the words *have, has,* or *had.*

Practice

Circle the correct form of the verb in each of the following sentences. The answers can be found at the end of the lesson.

1. The coach just (blow, blew, blown) the whistle for the fourth time.

2. Mr. Marks has not (do, did, done) a very good job of communicating with the staff.

3. The snow (come, came) very early this winter.

4. Louise had already (speak, spoke, spoken) to the insurance agent several times.

5. The buzzer will (ring, rang, rung) when it is time to enter the room.

6. Has your department (go, went, gone) to lunch?

7. Jason (see, saw, seen) the car leaving the parking area.

8. The city has not yet (begin, began, begun) the new recycling program

9. Olivia couldn't believe that she had actually (forget, forgot, forgotten) the key to her office again.

10. Jonathan was very nervous when he (take, took, taken) his place at the podium.

▶ Consistent Verb Tense

The tense of a verb tells when an action occurs, occurred, or will occur. Verbs have three basic tenses: present, past, and future. It's important to keep verb tenses consistent as you write. A passage that begins in present tense should continue in present tense. If it begins in past tense, it should stay in past tense. Do not mix tenses.

Wrong:
Dan **opened** the car door and **looks** for his briefcase.
Correct:
Dan **opened** the car door and **looked** for his briefcase.
Wrong:
When we **increase** maintenance services, we **reduced** repair costs.
Correct:
When we **increase** maintenance services, we **reduce** repair costs.

However, sometimes a writer must show that an action occurred at another time regardless of the tense in which the passage was begun. To allow this, each of these three tenses has three subdivisions: progressive, perfect, and progressive perfect.

Present Tense Forms

Present tense shows action that happens now or action that happens routinely. The *present progressive* tense shows an action happening now. An auxiliary verb (*am, is,* or *are*) precedes the –ing form (progressive form) of the verb. The *present perfect* tense shows an action that began in the past. An auxiliary verb (*have* or *has*) precedes the past participle form of the verb. The *present perfect progressive* tense also shows action that began in the past and is continuing in the present. Auxiliary verbs (*have been* or *has been*) precede the verb written in its –ing form (progressive form).

PRESENT TENSE			
PRESENT	**PROGRESSIVE**	**PERFECT**	**PERFECT PROGRESSIVE**
shows action happening now	shows action continuing now	shows action that began in the past	shows action that began in the past, continues now
Activists *lobby* for change.	Activists *are lobbying* for change.	Activists *have lobbied* for change.	Activists *have been lobbying* for change.
Sulfur *pollutes* the air.	Sulfur *is polluting* the air.	Sulfur *has polluted* the air.	Sulfur *has been polluting* the air.

All the above present tense forms can be used together without constituting a shift in tense. Look at the following paragraph to see how this is done. The verbs are highlighted, and the brackets identify the tense.

I **am writing** [present progressive] to protest the condition of the Mississippi River, from which our city **draws** [present] its drinking water. For years, industrial waste **has polluted** [present perfect] its waters, and officials **pay** [present] little attention to the problem. People who live near the river **have been lobbying** [present perfect progressive] for protective legislation, but their efforts **have failed** [present perfect]. I **want** [present] safe water to drink.

Past Tense Forms

Past tense shows action that happened in the past. It uses the past form of the verb. The *past progressive* tense shows a continuing action in the past. An auxiliary verb (*was* or *were*) precedes the progressive (*–ing*) form of the verb. The *past perfect* tense shows an action completed in the past or completed before some other past action. The auxiliary verb *had* precedes the past participle form of the verb. The *past perfect progressive* tense shows continuing action that began in the past. The auxiliary verbs *had been* precede the progressive form of the verb.

All the below past tense forms can be used together in writing a passage without constituting a shift in tense. The paragraph on the next page illustrates how this is done. The verbs are highlighted for you, and the brackets identify the tense.

PAST TENSE			
PAST	**PROGRESSIVE**	**PERFECT**	**PERFECT PROGRESSIVE**
occurred in the past	continuing action in the past	completed prior to another action	continuing action started in the past
Local officials *spoke* to the management.	Local officials *were speaking* to the management.	Local officials *had spoken* to the management.	Local officials *had been speaking* to the management.
The reporter *covered* the meetings.	The reporter *was covering* the meetings.	The reporter *had covered* the meetings.	The reporter *had been covering* the meetings.

Last year, local officials **cited** [past] a manufacturing company in our county for improperly disposing of hazardous waste. The company **ignored** [past] the action and **continued** [past] to dump its waste as they **had been doing** [past perfect progressive]. They **had dumped** [past perfect] waste the same way for years and **planned** [past] to continue. Several months later, the residue **seeped** [past] into the drinking water supply. A local environmentalist, who **had been tracking** [past perfect progressive] the company's dumping procedures, alerted local officials. They fined the company $3,000 for damages, but the company **has** never **paid** [past perfect] the fine.

Future Tense Forms

Future tense shows action that has yet to happen. The auxiliary verbs *will, would,* or *shall* precede the present form of the verb. The *future progressive* tense shows continuing actions in the future. The auxiliary verb phrases *will be, shall be,* or *would be* precede the progressive form of the verb. The *future perfect* tense shows actions that will be completed at a certain time in the future. The auxiliary verb phrases *will have, would have,* or *will have been* precede the past participle form of the verb. The *future perfect progressive* tense shows continuing actions that will be completed at a certain time in the future. The verb phrases *will have been, would have been,* or *shall have been* precede the progressive form of the verb.

All the future tense forms on the table below can be used together in writing a paragraph. They do not constitute a shift in tense. The following paragraph illustrates how this is done. The verbs are highlighted for you, and the brackets identify the tense.

Starting next week, we **will reduce** [future] the money we spend on waste disposal. We **will do** [future] this because our public relations costs have skyrocketed during the year. Since no one in the community **will sell** [future] land to us to use for waste disposal, we **will be relocating** [future progressive] in a new community with a better business environment. This move **would put** [future] over three hundred employees out of work. It **would reduce** [future] the amount of consumer dollars spent at local businesses.

By this time next year, nearly one thousand people **will have lost** [future perfect] their jobs. Your business leaders **will have been looking** [future perfect progressive] for ways to replace lost revenue. Furthermore, legislators **will be meddling** [future progressive] in our local affairs, and the news media **will have portrayed** [future perfect] us all as fools.

FUTURE TENSE			
FUTURE	**PROGRESSIVE**	**PERFECT**	**PERFECT PROGRESSIVE**
action that will happen	**continuing action that will happen**	**action that will be completed by a certain time**	**continuing action that will be completed by a certain time**
We *will begin* a letter-writing campaign.	Everyone *will be writing* letters.	By summer, we *will have written* reams of letters.	Legislators *will have been receiving* letters throughout the year.
Newspapers *will cover* this case.	Newspapers *will be covering* this case.	By summer, every newspaper *will have written* about this case.	Newspapers *will have been covering* the case throughout the year.

How Verb Tenses Convey Meaning

Managing verb tense carefully helps writers avoid the confusion that comes with thoughtless use. These examples illustrate how verb tense can completely change the meaning of a sentence.

Example:
> Beth discovered that Nick had left work and gone home.
> Beth discovered that Nick had left work and went home.

In the first sentence, because *gone* is the participle form, it goes with *had left* in the second part of the sentence. So Nick is the one who *had gone* home. In the second sentence, *went* is in the simple past tense like *discovered* in the first part of the sentence. So this time, it's Beth who *went* home.

Example:
> Cory told the officer that she had answered the phone and drank a can of soda pop.
> Cory told the officer that she had answered the phone and had drunk a can of soda pop.

In the first sentence, *drank* is in the same tense as *told*—they're both past tense. So Cory was drinking around the same time as she was telling. In the second sentence, *had drunk* matches *had answered,* so in this case, Cory was drinking around the time she answered the phone.

Have, not Of

When forming the various perfect tenses, people sometimes write *of* when they should write *have,* probably because they are writing what they hear. *I should've* (*should've* is a contraction of *should have*) sounds a lot like *I should of.* But the proper form in writing is *have,* not *of.*

Wrong:
> I **could of** seen the difference if I had looked more closely.

Correct:
> I **could have** seen the difference if I had looked more closely.

Wrong:
> The park ranger **should of** warned the campers about the bears.

Correct:
> The park ranger **should have** warned the campers about the bears.

Switching Verb Tenses

Sometimes, you have to switch from past tense to present to avoid implying an untruth.

Wrong:
> I met the new technician. He **was** very personable. [What happened? Did he die?]

Correct:
> I met the new technician. He **is** very personable.

Wrong:
> We went to the new Italian restaurant on Vine last night. The atmosphere **was** wonderful. [What happened? Did it burn down during the night?]

Correct:
> We went to the new Italian restaurant on Vine last night. The atmosphere **is** wonderful.

Even if a passage is written in past tense, a statement that continues to be true is written in present tense.

Examples:
> During Galileo's time, few people **believed** [past] that the Earth **revolves** [present] around the sun.
> The building engineer **explained** [past] to the plumber that the pipes **run** [present] parallel to the longest hallway in the building.

▶ Subjunctive Mood

When Tevya in *Fiddler on the Roof* sings, "If I were a rich man. . . ," he uses the verb *were* to signal that he is, in fact, not a rich man. Normally, the verb *was* would be used with the subject *I*, but *were* serves a special purpose. This is called the subjunctive *were*. It indicates a condition that is contrary to fact.

Examples:
If I **were** a cat, I could sleep all day long and never have to worry about work.
If he **were** more attentive to details, he could be a copy editor.

Practice
Circle the correct verb form in each of the following sentences.

11. Before I opened the door, I (ring, rang, had rung) the doorbell.

12. By the time I get to Phoenix, he will (read, have read) my goodbye letter.

13. The scientist explained why Saturn (is, was) surrounded by rings.

14. I would ask for a transfer if I (was, were) you.

15. The leaves on the trees have already (begin, began, begun) to fall.

16. The doctor took my pulse and (measures, measured) my blood pressure.

17. The president wishes he would (of, have) taken a stock option rather than a salary increase.

18. Boswick wishes he would have ordered a bigger sweatshirt because his (is, was) too small.

19. Ms. Grey announced that the floor manager (is, was) responsible for work schedules.

20. We could cut transportation costs if the plant (was, were) closer to the retail outlets.

▶ Answers

1. blew
2. done
3. came
4. spoken
5. ring
6. gone
7. saw
8. begun
9. forgotten
10. took
11. had rung
12. have read
13. is
14. were
15. begun
16. measured
17. have
18. is
19. is
20. were

Skill Building until Next Time

Listen carefully to people today. Do you hear common errors such as "I *could of* gone out if I had done my work"? Once you make it a habit to listen for verb choice errors, you'll realize how many people make them. Some mistakes are so accepted that they might not sound strange at first. The more sensitive you are to grammatical errors, the less likely you'll be to make them yourself—in both writing and speaking.

Using Verbs to Create Strong Writing

LESSON SUMMARY

If verbs drive meaning, lively verbs really make your writing accelerate. This lesson shows you how to use verbs to capture readers' interest.

Few people bother to read uninteresting writing. Even if they read it, they may not absorb the message. This lesson discusses ways to use verbs that will make your writing lively and interesting for the reader. Read the two paragraphs on the next page. Which one seems livelier, more interesting? The paragraphs tell an identical story, but one of them uses verbs effectively to tell the story in such a way that it is more likely to be remembered. The sentences are presented one at a time, side by side, so you can make the comparison more easily.

PARAGRAPH 1	PARAGRAPH 2
When my brother was asked by the local Rotary Club to speak to them about computer programming, our entire family was amazed by the request.	When the local Rotary Club asked my brother to speak to them about computer programming, the request amazed our entire family.
A gasp was made by mother, a laugh was emitted by my father, and my head was shaken by me.	My mother gasped, my father laughed, and I just shook my head.
My brother is considered by us to be a shy, quiet computer nerd.	We consider my brother a shy, quiet computer nerd.
Since I am regarded by my family as the creative one, I was assigned by my brother the task of creating the visual aids.	Since everyone in the family regards me as the creative one, my brother assigned me the task of creating the visual aids.
The information was organized by my father.	My father organized the information.
Formal invitations were requested by my mother from the Rotary Club secretary and were sent by her to all of our friends.	My mother requested formal invitations from the Rotary Club secretary and sent them to all of our friends.
Organizing and rehearsing of the presentation was worked on by my family until 10:00 P.M. the night before the presentation.	Our family organized and prepared until 10:00 P.M. the night before the presentation.
The fact that he was ready was known by us.	We knew he was ready.
That night, three feet of snow was dumped by the skies. The city was paralyzed, and all work and activities were canceled, including the Rotary Club meeting and my brother's presentation.	That night, the skies dumped three feet of snow, paralyzing the city and causing all work and activities to be canceled, including the Rotary Club meeting and my brother's presentation.

▶ Active vs. Passive Voice

When the subject of a sentence performs the action of the verb, we say the sentence is active. Write using active verbs to make your writing more conversational and interesting. In a sentence with an active verb, the person or thing that performs the action is named before the verb, or the action word(s), in a sentence. This may sound confusing, but the following examples illustrate the difference. The italicized words show who is performing the action. The underlined words are verbs.

PASSIVE VERBS	ACTIVE VERBS
I <u>was taken</u> to my first horse show by my *grandfather*.	My *grandfather* <u>took</u> me to my first horse show.
I <u>was taught</u> to fish by my *mother* almost before I <u>was taught</u> to walk.	My *mother* <u>taught</u> me to fish almost before *I* <u>learned</u> to walk.

In each of the active verb sentences, the person performing the action is named first. If you look more closely at these examples, you'll notice that the active verb versions are shorter and clearer. They sound more like natural conversation. Strive for these qualities in your writing. The following table illustrates the difference between active and passive voice in several of the verb tenses you learned in Lesson 10.

Most writers prefer active voice to passive voice because it makes the writing active and more alive. Generally, readers find active writing easier to read and remember. In this table and the one on page 92, you can see that active voice sentences tend to be shorter than passive ones.

VERB TENSE	ACTIVE VOICE	PASSIVE VOICE
Present	The *clerk* <u>opens</u> the mail.	The mail <u>is opened</u> by the *clerk*.
Past	The *clerk* <u>opened</u> the mail.	The mail <u>was opened</u> by the *clerk*.
Future	The *clerk* <u>will open</u> the mail.	The mail <u>will be opened</u> by the *clerk*.
Present Perfect	The *clerk* <u>has opened</u> the mail.	The mail <u>has been opened</u> by the *clerk*.
Past Perfect	The *clerk* <u>had opened</u> the mail.	The mail <u>had been opened</u> by the *clerk*.
Future Perfect	The *clerk* <u>will have opened</u> the mail.	The mail <u>will have been opened</u> by the *clerk*.

Practice

Choose the sentence written in active voice from each of the following sets. The answers to each set of questions can be found at the end of the lesson.

1. a. Talia quickly decorated the cake.
  b. The cake was quickly decorated by Talia.

2. a. The books were written by Mark Phillips.
  b. Mark Phillips wrote the books.

3. a. Three new members were introduced by the committee.
  b. The committee introduced three new members.

4. a. The shrubs will be planted by the gardener.
  b. The gardener will plant the shrubs.

5. a. The staff believes that management does not provide adequate benefits for new employees.
  b. It is believed by the staff that adequate benefits for new employees are not provided by the management.

6. a. The company barbecue is often planned by the accounting department.
  b. The accounting department often plans the company barbecue.

7. a. Every summer, thousands of tourists will visit the island.
  b. Every summer, the island will be visited by thousands of tourists.

When to Use Passive Voice

In addition to lacking life, the passive voice can also signal an unwillingness to take responsibility for actions or an intention to discourage questioning. The following sentence illustrates this:

> It has been recommended that twenty workers be laid off within the next three months.

The passive voice here is intended to make a definite statement of fact, one that will not be questioned. It leaves no loose ends. Dictators often write and speak in passive voice. A thoughtful person will see past the passive voice and ask questions anyway. Who is recommending this action? Why? Who will be doing the laying off? How will workers be chosen?

Passive voice is not always bad, however. Sometimes, though rarely, it actually works better than active voice. The following are situations when passive voice is preferable to active voice.

1. **When the object is more important than the agent of action (the doer)**
   Sometimes, in scientific writing, the object is the focus rather than the doer. The following paragraph is written in both passive and active voice, respectively. The first paragraph is more appropriate in this case because the operation, not the doctor, is the focus of the action. The passage cannot be written in active voice without placing the emphasis on the doer, the doctor. Therefore, passive voice is the better choice in this instance.

Passive voice:
> The three-inch incision is made right above the pubic bone. Plastic clips are used to clamp off blood vessels and minimize bleeding. The skin is folded back and secured with clamps. Next, the stomach muscle is cut at a fifteen-degree angle, right top to bottom left.

Active voice:
> The doctor makes a three-inch incision right above the pubic bone. He uses plastic clips to clamp off the blood vessels and minimize bleeding. He folds back the skin and secures it with clamps. Next, he cuts the stomach muscle at a fifteen-degree angle, right top to bottom left.

2. **When the agent of action (doer) is unknown or secret**
   Sometimes, a newswriter will protect a source by writing, "It was reported that . . ." In other instances, perhaps no one knows who perpetrated an action: "First State Bank was robbed . . ."

3. **When passive voice results in shorter sentences without detracting from the meaning**
   Generally, active voice is shorter and more concise than passive voice. However, there are a few exceptions. Examine the examples in the following table. If using passive voice saves time and trouble, in addition to resulting in a shorter sentence, use it.

ACTIVE	PASSIVE
The designers of the study told the interviewer to give interviewees an electric shock each time they smiled.	The interviewer was told to give the interviewees an electric shock each time they smiled.
The police apprehended Axtell, the detectives interrogated him, and the grand jury indicted him.	Axtell was apprehended, interrogated, and indicted.

▶ Other Life-Draining Verb Constructions

If thought is a train, then verbs are the wheels that carry the cargo along. The thought will move more quickly if it is transported by many big, strong wheels. Here are some constructions to avoid as well as suggestions for choosing bigger, better verbs.

Using State-of-Being Verbs

State-of-being verbs are all the forms of *be: am, is, are, was, were,* and so on. State-of-being verbs don't do as much as action verbs to move meaning. In our train-of-thought analogy, state-of-being verbs are very tiny wheels, incapable of moving big thoughts quickly or easily. If you have only trivial things to say, by all means, use state-of-being verbs. If your ideas are more complex or interesting, they will require bigger and better verbs.

Look at the following paragraphs. In the first version, most of the verbs are state-of-being verbs. In the second version, action verbs make the paragraph more interesting.

State-of-being verbs:

The class was outside during noon recess. The sunshine was bright. Earlier in the day, there was rain, but later, the weather was pleasant. The breeze was slight; the newly fallen leaves were in motion. Across the street from the school was an ice cream truck. It was what the children were looking at longingly.

Action verbs:

The class played outside during noon recess. The sun shone brightly. Earlier in the day, rain had fallen, but later, pleasant weather arrived. A slight breeze blew the newly fallen leaves. The children looked longingly at the ice cream truck across the street.

Turning Verbs into Nouns

Naturally, if you take the wheels off the train of thought and put them on a flatbed as cargo, the train will not move as well. Look at the following two sentences. In the first one, several verbs have been turned into nouns to make the writing sound "intellectual." This "verbification" actually makes the writing more difficult to read. The second sentence communicates the same information with the same amount of sophistication, but turning the nouns back into verbs makes it easier to read. Verb forms are highlighted to make them easier to identify.

The customer service division **is** now conducting an assessment of its system for the reaction to consumer concerns and the development of new products.

The customer service division **is assessing** its system for **reacting** to consumer concerns and **developing** new products.

Adding Unnecessary Auxiliary Verbs

Generally, if you don't need an auxiliary verb (*have, had, is, are, was, were, will, would,* and so on) to carry meaning (see Lesson 10), don't use one.

UNNESSARY AUXILIARY VERBS	CORRECTED VERSION
After lunch, we *would meet* in the lounge.	After lunch, we *met* in the lounge.
The temperature *was rising* steadily.	The temperature *rose* steadily.
Every morning, the doors *will open* at 8:00.	Every morning, the doors *open* at 8:00.

Starting with *There* or *It*

Many sentences unnecessarily begin with *there is/are/was/were* or with *it is/was*. Usually, all those words do is postpone the beginning of the actual thought. The following sentences illustrate how these life-draining words can be removed from your writing.

UNNECESSARY *THERE* OR *IT*	CORRECTED VERSION
There are three people who are authorized to use this machinery.	Three people are authorized to use this machinery.
There is one good way to handle this problem: to ignore it.	One good way to handle this problem is to ignore it.
It was a perfect evening for a rocket launch.	The evening was perfect for a rocket launch.
There were several people standing in line waiting for the bus.	Several people stood in line waiting for the bus.

▶ Use Lively, Interesting Verbs

If you want to move thought efficiently, work for precision and look for verbs that create an image in the reader's mind. Compare the sentences below to see this principle in action.

DULL	LIVELY
At my barbershop, someone does your nails and your shoes while your hair is being cut.	At my barbershop, someone manicures your nails and shines your shoes as your hair is cut.
Violent cartoons are harmful to children's emotional development and sense of reality.	Violent cartoons stunt children's emotional development and distort their sense of reality.

Practice

Choose the best sentence from each set. Keep in mind what you have learned about verbs in this lesson.

8. a. Incredibly useful feedback was given by the committee members about the proposed fundraiser.
b. The committee members gave incredibly useful feedback about the proposed fundraiser.

9. a. The party was thrown by two relatives and one friend.
b. Two relatives and one friend threw the party.

10. a. Those who hire customer service representatives think that excellent phone manner is more important than previous work experience.
b. Those responsible for the hiring of customer service representatives have a greater consideration for the manner in which applicants speak on the phone than they do for the work experience they bring to the job.

11. a. There are three rules that you should follow when you play this game.
 b. You should follow three rules when you play this game.

12. a. After breakfast every morning, we would pack our lunch.
 b. We packed our lunch every morning after breakfast.

13. a. Marisa smiled widely when she opened the door.
 b. Marisa was happy when she opened the door.

14. a. The applicant must have excellent programming skills.
 b. It is necessary for the applicant to have excellent programming skills.

▶ Answers

1. a.
2. b.
3. b.
4. b.
5. a.
6. b.
7. a.
8. b.
9. b.
10. a.
11. b.
12. b.
13. a.
14. a.

Skill Building until Next Time

As you read newspapers, magazines, textbooks, or other materials today, look for examples of sentences in active voice and in passive voice. Try converting some passive voice sentences into active voice and vice versa. Which version is more effective?

Subject-Verb Agreement

LESSON SUMMARY

Without thinking about it, you usually make sure your subjects and verbs agree, both in speaking and in writing. Only a few situations cause difficulty in subject-verb agreement. This lesson will show you how to deal with those few situations in your writing.

When a subject in a clause—the person or thing doing the action—matches the verb in number, we say the subject and verb *agree*. Most native English speakers have little trouble matching subjects with the correct verbs. A few grammatical constructions pose most of the problems. This lesson explains the concept of subject-verb agreement and provides practice in those problem areas.

▶ Agreement between Noun Subjects and Verbs

In written language, a subject must agree with its verb in number. In other words, if a subject is singular, the verb must be singular. If the subject is plural, the verb must be plural. If you are unsure whether a verb is singular or plural, apply this simple test. Fill in the blanks in the two sentences that follow with the matching form of the verb. The verb form that best completes the first sentence is singular. The verb form that best completes the second sentence is plural.

Singular

One person _____ .

Plural

Two people _____ .

Look at these examples using the verbs *speak, do,* and *was.* Try it yourself with any verb that confuses you. Unlike nouns, verbs ending in *s* are usually singular.

SINGULAR	PLURAL
One person <u>speaks</u>.	Two people <u>speak</u>.
One person <u>does</u>.	Two people <u>do</u>.
One person <u>was</u>.	Two people <u>were</u>.

Special Problems
Doesn't/Don't and Wasn't/Weren't

Some people have particular trouble with *doesn't/don't* (contractions for *does not* and *do not*) and with *wasn't/weren't* (contractions for *was not* and *were not*). *Doesn't* and *wasn't* are singular; *don't* and *weren't* are plural. If you say the whole phrase instead of the contraction, you'll usually get the right form.

Phrases Following the Subject

Pay careful attention to the subject in a sentence. Do not allow a phrase following it to mislead you into using a verb that does not agree with the subject. The subjects and verbs are highlighted in the following examples.

> **One** of the print orders **is** missing.
> The software **designs** by Liu Chen **are** complex and colorful.
> A **handbook** with thorough instructions **comes** with this product.
> The **president**, along with her three executive assistants, **leaves** for the conference tomorrow.

Special Singular Subjects

Some nouns are singular even though they end in *s*. Despite the plural form, they require a singular verb because we think of them as a single thing. Most of the nouns in the following list are singular. Some can be either singular or plural, depending on their use in the sentence.

measles	mathematics
mumps	civics
news	athletics
checkers	sports
marbles (the game)	politics
physics	statistics
economics	

Here are some examples of how these words work in sentences.

> The **news is** on at 6:00.
> **Checkers is** my favorite game.
> **Sports is** a healthy way to reduce stress.
> Low-impact **sports are** recommended for older adults.

Words stating a single amount or a time require a singular verb. Examine a sentence carefully to see if the amount or time is considered a single measure.

> Two dollars **is** the price of that small replacement part. [single amount]
> Two dollars **are** lying on my dresser.
> Three hours **was** required to complete this simulation. [single measure]
> Three hours of each day **were** spent rehearsing.
> Three-quarters of her time **is** spent writing.

Practice

Circle the correct verb in each of the following sentences. The answers to each set of questions can be found at the end of the lesson.

1. When the clown (performs, perform), the children in the audience (laughs, laugh).

2. Claire (vacations, vacation) in Maine, but her parents (vacations, vacation) in Florida.

3. The hostess (greets, greet) the customers while the busboys (clears, clear) the tables.

4. Luigi (speaks, speak) English, but his parents (speaks, speak) Italian.

5. The bakery (wasn't, weren't) open on Sunday afternoon.

6. The new tenants (doesn't, don't) pay their rent on time.

7. The percussionist (drums, drum) loudly while the dancers (performs, perform).

8. The box office (doesn't, don't) sell tickets until the week before the show.

9. The office was closed yesterday because the heat (wasn't, weren't) working.

10. Marly (doesn't, don't) know if the neighbors (is, are) on vacation.

11. The milk, along with the eggs, (is, are) added to the batter before baking.

12. These statistics (is, are) not at all what we expected.

13. Statistics (was, were) a required course at my university.

14. One of the students (is, are) looking for the stack of books that (was, were) misplaced.

15. Half of the banana (was, were) eaten.

16. Half of the bananas (was, were) eaten.

▶ Agreement between Pronoun Subjects and Verbs

Pronoun subjects present a problem for even the most sophisticated speakers of English. Some pronouns are always singular; others are always plural. A handful of pronouns can be either singular or plural.

Singular Pronouns

These pronouns are always singular.

each	anyone	nobody
either	everybody	one
neither	everyone	somebody
anybody	no one	someone

The pronouns in the first column are the ones most likely to be misused. You can avoid a mismatch by mentally adding the word *one* after the pronoun and removing the other words between the pronoun and the verb. Look at the following examples to see how this is done.

Each of the men wants his own car.
Each *one* wants his own car.
Either of the salesclerks knows where the sale merchandise is located.
Either *one* knows where the sale merchandise is located.

QUESTION FORM	STATEMENT FORM
(Is, Are) some of the customers noticing the difference?	Some of the customers **are** noticing the difference.
(Has, Have) either of the shipments arrived?	Either [*one*] of the shipments **has** arrived.
(Does, Do) each of the terminals have a printer?	Each [*one*] of the terminals **does** have a printer.

These sentences may sound awkward because so many speakers misuse these pronouns, and you have probably become accustomed to hearing them used incorrectly. Despite that, the substitution trick (*one* for the words following the pronoun) will help you avoid this mistake.

Watch Out for Questions

With questions beginning with *has* or *have*, remember that *has* is singular while *have* is plural. Pay special attention to the verb-subject combination in a question. In fact, the correct verb is easier to identify if you turn the question into a statement.

Plural Pronouns

These pronouns are always plural and require a plural verb.

both	many
few	several

Singular/Plural Pronouns

The following pronouns can be either singular or plural. The words or prepositional phrases following them determine whether they are singular or plural. If the phrase following the pronoun contains a plural noun or pronoun, the verb must be plural. If the phrase following the pronoun contains a singular noun or pronoun, the verb must be singular. See how this is done in the sentences following the list of pronouns. The key words are highlighted.

all	none
any	some
most	

SINGULAR	PLURAL
All of the **work is** finished.	**All** of the **jobs are** finished.
Is any of the **pizza** left?	**Are** any of the **pieces** of pizza left?
Most of the **grass has** turned brown.	**Most** of the **blades** of grass **have** turned brown.
None of the **time was** wasted.	**None** of the **minutes were** wasted.
Some of the **fruit was** spoiled.	**Some** of the **apples were** spoiled.

Practice

Circle the correct verb in each of the following sentences. Answers are at the end of the lesson.

17. Neither of these solutions (addresses, address) the primary problem.

18. Each of the letters (makes, make) a strong case for changing the policy.

19. Some of the applicants (was, were) unhappy with the new job description.

20. All of the recommendations (has, have) been made.

21. Either of these software programs (is, are) suitable for my staff.

22. (Was, Were) any of the parts missing?

23. (Has, Have) either of the owners expressed an interest in selling the property?

24. (Do, Does) each of the cars have valid registrations?

25. Neither of our largest accounts (needs, need) to be serviced at this time.

26. Both of the applicants (seems, seem) qualified.

27. A woman in one of my classes (works, work) at the Civic Center box office.

28. None of our resources (goes, go) to outside consultants.

29. A good knowledge of the rules (helps, help) you understand the game.

30. Each of these prescriptions (causes, cause) bloating and irritability.

31. (Have, Has) either of them ever arrived on time?

▶ Special Sentence Structures

Compound Subjects

- If two nouns or pronouns are joined by *and*, they require a plural verb.

    He and she **want** to buy a new house.
    Jack and Jill **want** to buy a new house.

- If two singular nouns or pronouns are joined by *or* or *nor*, they require a singular verb. Think of them as two separate sentences and you'll never make a mistake in agreement.

    Jack or Jill **wants** to buy a new house.
    Jack **wants** to buy a new house.
    Jill **wants** to buy a new house.

- Singular and plural subjects joined by *or* or *nor* require a verb that agrees with the subject closest to the verb.

    Neither management nor the **employees like** the new agreement.
    Neither the employees nor the **management likes** the new agreement.

Make Sure You Find the Subject

Verbs agree with the subject, not the complement, of a sentence. The verb, a form of *be*, links the subject and the complement, but usually, the subject comes first and the complement comes after the verb.

Taxes were the main challenge facing the financial department.
The main **challenge** facing the financial department **was** taxes.
A serious **problem** for most automobile commuters **is** traffic jams.
Traffic jams are a serious problem for most automobile commuters.

Questions and Sentences Beginning with *There* or *Here*

When a sentence asks a question or begins with the words *there* or *here*, the subject follows the verb. Locate the subject of the sentence and make certain the verb matches it. In the following examples, the subjects and verbs are highlighted in the corrected forms.

WRONG	CORRECTED
What is the conditions of the contract?	What **are** the **conditions** of the contract?
Why is her reports always so disorganized?	Why **are** her **reports** always so disorganized?
Here's the records you requested.	Here **are** the **records** you requested.
There is four people seeking this promotion.	There **are** four **people** seeking this promotion.

Inverted Sentences

Inverted sentences also contain subjects that follow, rather than precede, the verbs. Locate the subject in the sentence and make certain the verb agrees with it. In the following example sentences, the subjects and verbs in the corrected sentences are highlighted.

WRONG	CORRECT
Beside the front desk stands three new vending machines.	Beside the front desk **stand** three new vending **machines**.
Suddenly, out of the thicket comes three large bucks.	Suddenly, out of the thicket **come** three large **bucks**.
Along with our highest recommendation goes our best wishes in your new job.	Along with our highest recommendation **go** our best **wishes** in your new job.

Practice

Circle the correct verb in each of the following sentences. Answers are at the end of the lesson.

32. Every other day, either Bert or Ernie (takes, take) out the trash.

33. Neither the style nor the color (matches, match) what we currently have.

34. Either the associates or the manager (orders, order) the merchandise.

35. Either the manager or the associates (orders, order) the merchandise.

36. (Is, Are) the men's wear or the women's wear department on the ground floor?

37. Mr. Jefson's passion (is, are) economics.

38. (Was, Were) there any furniture sets left over after the sale?

39. There (isn't, aren't) many days left before the grand opening.

40. Here (is, are) the information you requested.

41. Off into the horizon (runs, run) the herd of buffalo.

▶ Answers

1. performs, laugh
2. vacations, vacation
3. greets, clear
4. speaks, speak
5. wasn't
6. don't
7. drums, perform
8. doesn't
9. wasn't
10. doesn't, are
11. is
12. are
13. was
14. is, was
15. was
16. were
17. addresses
18. makes
19. were
20. have
21. is

22. Were
23. Has
24. Does
25. needs
26. seem
27. works
28. go
29. helps
30. causes
31. Has
32. takes
33. matches
34. orders
35. order
36. Is
37. is
38. Were
39. aren't
40. is
41. runs

Skill Building until Next Time

Listen to people as they speak. Do they use verbs correctly? Do they use the correct tense? Do the subjects and verbs match? It's probably not a good idea to correct your family, friends, and coworkers, but you can give yourself some good practice by listening for mistakes.

13 ▶ Using Pronouns

LESSON SUMMARY

Pronouns are so often *misused* in speech that many people don't really know how to avoid pronoun errors in writing. This lesson shows you how to avoid the most common ones.

A *pronoun* is a word used in place of a noun. Misused pronouns call attention to themselves and detract from the message of a piece of writing. This lesson explains the basic principles of pronoun use and highlights the most common pronoun problems: agreement, case, noun-pronoun pairs, incomplete constructions, ambiguous pronoun references, and reflexive pronouns.

▶ Pronouns and Antecedents

The noun represented by a pronoun is called its *antecedent*. The prefix *ante–* means *to come before*. Usually, the antecedent comes before the pronoun in a sentence. In the following examples, the pronouns are italicized and the antecedents (the words they represent) are underlined.

The government <u>workers</u> received *their* paychecks.
<u>Jane</u> thought *she* saw the missing <u>boy</u> and reported *him* to the police.
The shift <u>supervisor</u> hates these <u>accidents</u> because *he* thinks *they* can be easily avoided.

A pronoun must match the number of its antecedent. In other words, if the antecedent is singular, the pronoun must also be singular. If the antecedent is plural, the pronoun must also be plural. Few people make mistakes when matching a pronoun with a noun antecedent. However, sometimes a pronoun is the antecedent for another pronoun. Indefinite pronoun antecedents frequently result in a number mismatch between pronoun and antecedent. In Lesson 12, you learned about singular pronouns. Here is the list again.

each	anyone	nobody
either	everybody	one
neither	everyone	somebody
anybody	no one	someone

- A pronoun with one of the words from this list as its antecedent must be singular.

    <u>Each</u> (singular) of the men brought *his* (singular) favorite snack to the picnic.

    <u>Everyone</u> (singular) who wants to be in the "Toughman" contest should pay up *his* (singular) life insurance.

    <u>Somebody</u> left *her* purse underneath the desk.

    <u>Neither</u> of the occupants could locate *his* (or *her*) key to the apartment.

- If two or more singular nouns or pronouns are joined by *and*, use a plural pronoun.

    <u>Buddha and Muhammad</u> built religions around *their* philosophies.

    If <u>he and she</u> want to know where I was, *they* should ask me.

- If two or more singular nouns or pronouns are joined by *or*, use a singular pronoun.

    <u>Matthew or Jacob</u> will loan you *his* calculator.

    The <u>elephant or the moose</u> will furiously protect *its* young.

- If a singular and a plural noun or pronoun are joined by *or*, the pronoun agrees with the closest noun or pronoun it represents.

    Neither the soldiers nor the <u>sergeant</u> was sure of *his* location.

    Neither the sergeant nor the <u>soldiers</u> were sure of *their* location.

Practice

Circle the correct pronoun in each of the following sentences. The answers to each set of questions can be found at the end of the lesson.

1. No one in (his, their) right mind would turn down that amazing job offer.

2. Anyone who wants to become a member should pay (her, their) dues by the last day of the month.

3. Neither the campers nor the counselor remembered to bring (his, their) compass.

4. Tell someone in the human resources department about your situation and (she, they) will speak to your supervisor.

5. If you order a sandwich or a salad, (it, they) will be ready in ten minutes.

6. Neither Lily nor Emily will volunteer (herself, themselves) to work late this evening.

7. Almost anybody can improve (her, their) public speaking skills by attending this workshop.

8. I met someone who offered (her, their) services to help organize the fundraising dinner.

9. When you want to impress a client, remember to send (him, them) a personalized thank you note.

▶ Pronoun Case

Most people know when to use *I*, when to use *me*, or when to use *my*. These three pronouns illustrate the three cases of the first-person singular pronoun: nominative (*I*), objective (*me*), and possessive (*my*). The following table shows the cases of all the personal pronouns, both singular and plural.

PERSONAL PRONOUN CASE		
NOMINATIVE	OBJECTIVE	POSSESSIVE
I	me	my
we	us	our
you	you	your
he	him	his
she	her	her
they	them	their
it	it	its

Nominative case pronouns (those in the first column) are used as subjects or as complements following linking verbs (*am, is, are, was, were*—any form of *be*). Nominative case pronouns following a linking verb may sound strange to you because so few people use them correctly.

> **They** left a few minutes early to mail the package. [subject]
> **I** looked all over town for the type of paper you wanted. [subject]
> The doctor who removed my appendix was **he**. [follows a linking verb]
> "This is **she**, or it is **I**," said Barbara into the phone. [follows a linking verb]
> The winners of the sales contest were **he** and **she**. [follows a linking verb]

Objective case pronouns (those in the middle column in the table) are used as objects following an action verb or as objects of a preposition.

> The help line representative gave **him** an answer over the phone. [follows an action verb]

> Of all these samples, I prefer **them**. [follows an action verb]
> We went to lunch with Sammy and **him**. [object of the preposition *with*]
> We couldn't tell whether the package was for **them** or **us**. [object(s) of the preposition *for*]

Possessive case pronouns (those in the third column in the table) show ownership. Few English speakers misuse the possessive case pronouns. Most pronoun problems occur with the nominative and objective cases.

Problems with Pronoun Case

A single pronoun in a sentence is easy to use correctly. In fact, most English speakers would readily identify the mistakes in the following sentences.

> **Me** worked on the project with **he**.
> My neighbor gave **she** a ride to work.

Most people know that **Me** in the first sentence should be **I** and that **he** should be **him**. They would also know that **she** in the second sentence should be **her**. Such errors are easy to spot when the pronouns are used alone in a sentence. The problem occurs when a pronoun is used with a noun or another pronoun. See if you can spot the errors in the following sentences.

Wrong:
> The grand marshall rode with Shane and I.
> Donna and me are going to the Civic Center.
> The stage manager spoke to my brother and I.

The errors in these sentences are harder to see than those in the sentences with a single pronoun. If you turn the sentence with two pronouns into two separate sentences, the error becomes very obvious.

Correct:
> The grand marshall rode with Shane.
> The grand marshall rode with **me**. (not *I*)
> Donna is going to the Civic Center. [Use the singular verb *is* in place of *are*.]
> **I** (not *me*) am going to the Civic Center. [Use the verb *am* in place of *are*.]
> The stage manager spoke to my brother.
> The stage manager spoke to **me**. (not *I*)

Splitting a sentence in two does not work as well with the preposition *between*. If you substitute *with* for *between*, then the error is easier to spot.

> The problem is between (she, her) and (I, me).
> The problem is with **her**. (not *she*)
> The problem is with **me**. (not *I*)

Practice

Circle the correct pronouns in the following sentences. Answers are at the end of the lesson.

10. Andy or Arvin will bring (his, their) camera so (he, they) can take pictures of the party.

11. Benny and (he, him) went to the movies with Bonnie and (I, me).

12. Neither my cousins nor my uncle knows what (he, they) will do tomorrow.

13. Why must it always be (I, me) who cleans up the lounge?

14. The pilot let (he, him) and (I, me) look at the instrument panel.

15. Have you heard the latest news about (she, her) and (they, them)?

16. My friend and (I, me) both want to move to another location.

▶ Noun-Pronoun Pairs

Sometimes, a noun is immediately followed by a pronoun in a sentence. To make certain you use the correct pronoun, delete the noun from the pair. Look at the following examples to see how this is done.

PRONOUNS IN NOUN-PRONOUN PAIRS	
WHICH PRONOUN?	**REMOVE THE NOUN**
(We, Us) support personnel wish to lodge a complaint.	**We** wish to lodge a complaint.
They gave the job to (we, us) inventory staffers.	They gave the job to **us**.
The committee threw (we, us) retirees a huge end-of-the-year party.	The committee threw **us** a huge end-of-the-year party.

▶ Incomplete Constructions

Sometimes, a pronoun comes at the end of a sentence following a comparative word such as *than* or *as*.

> Harold spent as much time on this project as (they, them).
> Duane can build cabinets better than (I, me).
> The long day exhausted us more than (they, them).
> My youngest child is now taller than (I, me).

In each of these sentences, part of the meaning is implied. To figure out which pronoun is correct, complete the sentence in your head and use the pronoun that makes more sense.

> Harold spent as much time on this project as *they did*.
> Harold spent as much time on this project as *he spent on them*.

The first sentence makes more sense, so *they* would be the correct choice.

> Duane can build cabinets better than *I can*.
> Duane can build cabinets better than *he can build me*.

The first sentence makes more sense, so *I* is the correct pronoun.

> The long day exhausted us more than *they did*.
> The long day exhausted us more than *it did them*.

The second sentence makes more sense, so *them* is the correct choice.

> My youngest child is now taller than *I am*.

There is no way to complete the sentence using the pronoun *me*, so *I* is the correct choice.

Pronoun choice is especially important if the sentence makes sense either way. The following sentence can be completed using both pronouns, either of which makes good sense. The pronoun choice controls the meaning. The writer must be careful to choose the correct pronoun if the meaning is to be accurately portrayed.

> I work with Assad more than (she, her).
> I work with Assad more than *she does*.
> I work with Assad more than *I work with her*.

Use the pronoun that portrays the intended meaning.

▶ Ambiguous Pronoun References

Sometimes, a sentence is written in such a way that a pronoun can refer to more than one antecedent. When this happens, we say the meaning is *ambiguous*. In the following examples, the ambiguous pronouns are italicized, and the possible antecedents are underlined.

> When <u>Eric</u> spoke to his girlfriend's <u>father</u>, *he* was very polite.
> Remove the <u>door</u> from the <u>frame</u> and paint *it*.
> <u>Jamie</u> told <u>Linda</u> *she* should be ready to go within an hour.
> <u>Pat</u> told <u>Craig</u> *he* had been granted an interview.

See how the sentences are rewritten below to clarify the ambiguous references.

> Eric was very polite when he spoke to his girlfriend's father.
> Paint the door after removing it from the frame.
> Jamie told Linda to be ready to go within an hour.
> Pat told Craig that Craig had been granted an interview.

▶ Improper Reflexive Pronouns

▶ Answers

A *reflexive pronoun* is one that includes the word *self* or *selves*: *myself, yourself, himself, herself, ourselves, themselves.* The following section explains ways in which reflexive pronouns are sometimes misused.

- The possessive pronouns *his* and *their* cannot be made reflexive.

  Wrong:

  They decided to do the remodeling theirselves.

  Mark wanted to arrange the meeting hisself.

  Correct:

  They decided to do the remodeling *themselves*.

  Mark wanted to arrange the meeting *himself*.

- Avoid using a reflexive pronoun when a personal pronoun works in the sentence.

  Wrong:

  Three associates and myself chose the architect for the building.

  The preliminary results of the poll were revealed only to ourselves.

  Correct:

  Three associates and *I* chose the architect for the building.

  The preliminary results of the poll were revealed only to *us.*

1. his
2. her
3. his
4. she
5. it
6. herself
7. her
8. her
9. him
10. his, he
11. he, me
12. he
13. I
14. him, me
15. her, them
16. I

Skill Building until Next Time

Identify the pronoun mistake or two that you make most often. In your conversation, make a conscious effort to use the pronouns correctly at least three times.

14▶ Problem Verbs and Pronouns

LESSON SUMMARY

Sit or *set*? *Your* or *you're*? *There* or *their*? Or is it *they're*? Knowing how to use such problem pairs is the mark of the educated writer. This lesson shows you how.

This lesson covers problem verbs such as *lie/lay, sit/set, rise/raise,* and their various forms. It also covers problem pronouns such as *its/it's, your/you're, whose/who's, who/that/which,* and *there/they're/their.* You can distinguish yourself as an educated writer if you can use these verbs and pronouns correctly in formal writing situations.

▶ Problem Verbs

Lie/Lay

Few people use *lie* and *lay* and their principal parts correctly, perhaps because few people know the difference in meaning between the two. The verb *lie* means *to rest or recline.* The verb *lay* means *to put or place.* The table on the next page shows the principal parts of each of these verbs. Their meanings, written in the correct form, appear in parentheses.

FORMS OF *LIE* AND *LAY*			
PRESENT	**PROGRESSIVE**	**PAST**	**PAST PARTICIPLE***
lie, lies	lying	lay	lain
(rest, rests)	(resting)	(rested)	(rested)
lay, lays	laying	laid	laid
(place, places)	(placing)	(placed)	(placed)

*The past participle is the form used with have, has, or had.

To choose the correct form of *lie* or *lay*, simply look at the meanings in parentheses. Choose the word in parentheses that makes the most sense and use the corresponding form of *lie* or *lay*. Sometimes, none of the words seem especially appropriate. Nevertheless, choose the option that makes more sense than any of the others. If a sentence contains the word *down*, mentally delete the word from the sentence to make the appropriate verb more obvious. Examine the sample sentences to see how this is done.

The garbage cans are _____ in the middle of the street. [Requires progressive]
Resting makes better sense than *placing*.
Choose *lying*.

Keith told Nan to _____ the mail on the dining room table. [Requires present]
Place makes better sense than *rest*.
Choose *lay*.

The sandwiches _____ in the sun for over an hour before we ate them. [Requires past]
Rested makes better sense than *placed*.
Choose *lay*.

Yesterday afternoon, I _____ down for an hour.
[Requires past]
Remove the word *down*.
Rested makes better sense than *placed*.
Choose *lay*.

Barry thought he had _____ the papers near the copy machine. [Requires past participle]
Placed makes better sense than *rested*.
Choose *laid*.

Practice

Write the correct form of *lie* or *lay* in each of the blanks that follow. Answers are at the end of the lesson.

1. After the alarm sounded, I _____ in bed for another hour.

2. _____ the packages on the mailroom floor.

3. The latest edition of the newspaper _____ on the desk.

4. The paper carrier _____ the latest edition of the newspaper on the desk.

5. No one had any idea how long the sandwiches had _____ in the sun or who had _____ them there in the first place.

Sit/Set

These two verbs are very similar to *lie* and *lay*. *Sit* means *to rest*. *Set* means *to put or place*. The following table shows the principal parts of each of these verbs. Their meanings, written in the correct form, appear in parentheses.

FORMS OF *SIT* AND *SET*			
PRESENT	**PROGRESSIVE**	**PAST**	**PAST PARTICIPLE***
sit, sits	sitting	sat	sat
(rest, rests)	(resting)	(rested)	(rested)
set, sets	setting	set	set
(put, place; puts, places)	(putting, placing)	(put, placed)	(put, placed)

*The past participle is the form used with have, has, or had.

Choose the correct form of *sit* or *set* by using the meanings (the words in parentheses) in the sentence first. Decide which meaning makes the most sense, and then choose the corresponding verb. See how this is done in the following examples.

> The speaker _____ the chair next to the podium.
> *Put* or *placed* makes more sense than *rested*.
> Choose *set*.
> The speaker _____ in the chair next to the podium.
> *Rested* makes more sense than *put* or *placed*.
> Choose *sat*.

Practice

Write the correct form of *sit* or *set* in each of the blanks that follow. Answers are at the end of the lesson.

6. The board of directors _____ aside additional money for research and development.

7. My desk is the one _____ closest to the fax machine.

8. I can't remember where I _____ the mail down.

9. I _____ down next to Jill and _____ my briefcase on the chair next to me.

10. We had _____ in the waiting room for almost an hour before the doctor saw us.

Rise/Raise

The verb *rise* means *to go up.* The verb *raise* means *to move something up. Raise* requires an object. In other words, something must receive the action of the verb raise (*raise your hand, raise the flag, raise the objection, raise children*). This table shows the principal parts of both verbs.

FORMS OF *RISE* AND *RAISE*			
PRESENT	**PROGRESSIVE**	**PAST**	**PAST PARTICIPLE***
rises, rise	rising	rose	risen
(goes up, go up)	(going up)	(went up)	(gone up)
(comes up, come up)	(coming up)	(came up)	(come up)
raises, raise	raising	raised	raised
(moves up, move up)	(moving up)	(moved up)	(moved up)

*The past participle is the form used with have, has, or had.

Choose the correct form of *rise* or *raise* by using the meanings (the words in parentheses) in the sentence first. Decide which meaning makes the most sense, and choose the corresponding verb. See how this is done in the following examples. Sometimes, none of the words seem especially appropriate. Nevertheless, choose the option that makes more sense than any of the others.

> The sun _____ a little bit earlier each day of the spring.
> *Comes up* makes the most sense.
> Choose *rises.*
> Without realizing it, we began to _____ our voices.
> *Move up* makes more sense than any of the other options.
> Choose *raise.*
> The river _____ over two feet in the last hour.
> *Went up* makes the most sense.
> Choose *rose.*

Practice

Write the correct form of *rise* or *raise* in each of the blanks that follow. Answers are at the end of the lesson.

11. The guard _____ the flag every morning before the sun _____.

12. The couple _____ seven of their own children and adopted three more.

13. By late morning the fog had _____ enough for us to see the neighboring farm.

14. The stockholders _____ from their chairs to _____ an objection.

► Problem Pronouns

Its/It's

Its is a possessive pronoun that means *belonging to it. It's* is a contraction for *it is* or *it has*. You will only use *it's* when you can also substitute the words *it is*. Take time to make this substitution, and you will never confuse these two words.

> A doe will hide **its** [belonging to the it—the doe] fawn carefully before going out to graze.
> **It's** [it is] time we packed up and moved to a new location.
> The new computer system has proven **its** [belonging to it] value.
> We'll leave the game as soon as **it's** [it is] over.

Your/You're

Your is a possessive pronoun that means *belonging to you. You're* is a contraction for the words *you are*. You will only use *you're* when you can also substitute the words *you are*. Take time to make this substitution, and you will never confuse these two words.

> Is this **your** [belonging to you] idea of a joke?
> As soon as **you're** [you are] finished, you may leave.
> **Your** [belonging to you] friends are the people you most enjoy.
> **You're** [you are] friends whom we value.

Whose/Who's

Whose is a possessive pronoun that means *belonging to whom. Who's* is a contraction for the words *who is* or *who has*. Take time to make this substitution, and you will never confuse these two words.

> **Who's** [Who is] in charge of the lighting for the show?
> **Whose** [belonging to whom] car was that?

This is the nurse **who's** [who is] on duty until morning.
Here is the man **whose** [belonging to whom] car I ran into this morning.

Who/That/Which

Who refers to people. *That* refers to things. *Which* is generally used to introduce nonrestrictive clauses that describe things. (See Lesson 4 for nonrestrictive clauses.) Look at the following sentences to see how each of these words is used.

> There is the woman **who** helped me fix my flat tire.
> The man **who** invented the polio vaccine died in 1995.
> This is the house **that** Jack built.
> The book **that** I wanted is no longer in print.
> Abigail, **who** rescued my cat from the neighbor's tree, lives across the street.
> Yassir Arafat, **who** heads the PLO, met with Israeli leaders.
> The teacher asked us to read *Lord of the Flies*, **which** is my favorite novel.
> Mt. Massive, **which** is the tallest peak in the Rocky Mountains, looms above Leadville, Colorado.

There/Their/They're

There is an adverb telling where an action or item is located. *Their* is a possessive pronoun that shows ownership. *They're* is a contraction for the words *they are*. Of all the confusing word groups, this one is misused most often. Here is an easy way to distinguish among these words.

■ Take a close look at this version of the word: t**HERE**. You can see that *there* contains the word *here*. Wherever you use the word *there*, you should be able to substitute the word *here*, and the sentence should still make sense.

■ *Their* means *belonging to them.* Of the three words, *their* can be most easily transformed into the word *them.* Try it. You'll discover that two short markings—connecting the *i* to the *r* and then drawing a line to make the *ir* into an *m*—will turn *their* into *them.* This clue will help you avoid misusing *their.*

■ Finally, imagine that the apostrophe in *they're* is actually a very small letter *a.* If you change *they're* to *they are* in a sentence, you'll never misuse the word. Look over the following example sentences.

> **There** [here] is my paycheck.
>
> The new chairs are in **there** [here].
>
> **Their** [belonging to them] time has almost run out.
>
> This is **their** [belonging to them] problem, not mine.
>
> **They're** [they are] planning to finish early in the morning.
>
> I wonder how **they're** [they are] going to work this out.

Practice

Circle the correct word in each set of parentheses below. Answers are at the end of the lesson.

15. Call her when (its, it's) time to go to lunch.

16. The company was known for (its, it's) excellent healthcare benefits.

17. (Its, It's) a ripe banana when (its, it's) peel is yellow instead of green.

18. Don't forget (your, you're) umbrella when you leave the house this morning.

19. (Your, You're) scheduled to meet with the new client tomorrow morning.

20. (Your, You're) schedule for tomorrow is finalized.

21. Don't forget to sign (your, you're) name in the guestbook if (your, you're) leaving.

22. This is the scarf (who, which, that) I borrowed from Jessica.

23. My friend Evan is the one (who, which, that) lives in Seattle.

24. The new grocery store, (who, which, that) is located in the center of town, is scheduled to open next week.

25. Georgia O'Keeffe, (who, which, that) is my favorite artist, lived in New Mexico for many years.

26. Do you know the person (who, which, that) lives in the apartment upstairs?

27. (There, Their, They're) scheduled to arrive in London next week.

28. (Your, You're) never going to find the books in (there, their, they're).

29. The teller (who, which, that) gave me the deposit slip is over (there, their, they're).

30. (Its, It's) been five years since (there, their, they're) apartment was painted.

31. (Who's, Whose) idea was it to throw a surprise party?

32. (Who's Whose) been handling the supply orders for our department?

33. (Who's, Whose) birthday is it?

34. Jacob met with the person (who's, whose) organizing the conference.

▶ Answers

1. lay
2. Lay
3. lay
4. laid
5. lain, laid
6. set
7. sitting
8. set
9. sat, set
10. sat
11. raised, rose *or* raises, rises
12. raised
13. risen
14. rose, raise
15. it's
16. its
17. It's, its
18. your
19. You're
20. Your
21. your, you're
22. that
23. who
24. which
25. who
26. who
27. They're
28. You're, there
29. who, there
30. It's, their
31. Whose
32. Who's
33. Whose
34. who's

Skill Building until Next Time

Identify the special verb or pronoun problem that gives you the most trouble. Explain the correct way to use it to a friend or family member. Make a conscious effort to use it correctly at least three times today.

15 ▶ Modifiers

LESSON SUMMARY

This lesson shows you how to avoid common problems with adjectives and adverbs.

Words and phrases that describe other words are called *modifiers*. Words that describe nouns and pronouns are called *adjectives*. Words that describe verbs, adjectives, or adverbs are called *adverbs*. Entire phrases or groups of words can also function as modifiers. The English language is structured in such a way that modifiers play a vital part in communication. Using them correctly is an important skill.

▶ Adjectives

Adjectives describe a noun or pronoun in a sentence. Here is an easy way to tell if a word is an adjective. Adjectives answer one of three questions about another word in the sentence: *which one? what kind?* and *how many?* The table on the next page illustrates this. The adjectives are highlighted to make them easy to identify.

ADJECTIVES		
WHICH ONE?	**WHAT KIND?**	**HOW MANY?**
that cubicle	**sports** car	**many** examples
the **other** arrangement	**red** stickers	**three** containers
our **first** project	**wise** mentor	**several** desks

Pay special attention to adjectives that follow linking verbs. Sometimes, the adjective follows a verb, but it describes a noun or pronoun that comes before the verb. The following sentences illustrate this. The italicized adjectives describe the underlined nouns.

> This <u>cheesecake</u> tastes *delicious*. [delicious cheesecake]
> Chris's <u>change</u> of heart seemed *appropriate*. [appropriate change]
> The <u>room</u> smelled *strange*. [strange room]

Fewer/Less, Number/Amount

Use the adjective *fewer* to modify plural nouns, things that can be counted. Use *less* for singular nouns that represent a quantity or a degree. Most nouns to which an *s* can be added require the adjective *fewer*.

> The promotional staff had **fewer** innovative ideas [plural noun] than the marketing staff.
> The marketing staff had **less** time [singular noun] to brainstorm than the promotional staff.

The same principle applies to the nouns *number* and *amount*. Use the noun *number* when referring to things that can be made plural or that can be counted. Use the noun *amount* when referring to singular nouns.

> The **number** of hours [plural noun] we have for this telethon has been reduced.
> The **amount** of time [singular noun] we have for this telethon has been reduced.

▶ Adverbs

Use adverbs to describe verbs, adjectives, and other adverbs. Here is an easy way to tell if a word is an adverb. Adverbs answer one of these questions about another word in the sentence: *where? when? how?* and *to what extent?* The following table illustrates this. The adverbs are highlighted.

ADVERBS			
WHERE?	**WHEN?**	**HOW?**	**TO WHAT EXTENT?**
The line moved **forward**.	I saw him **yesterday**.	They spoke **softly**.	I could **hardly** understand.
Store your gear **below**.	Come around **later**.	Cindy types **quickly**.	You **narrowly** missed that car.
Stand **here**.	We'll talk **tonight**.	He sang **happily**.	We **still** won't give in.

This next table shows examples of adverbs modifying verbs, adjectives, and other adverbs. The adverbs are highlighted; the words they modify are underlined.

ADVERBS THAT MODIFY		
VERBS	**ADJECTIVES**	**OTHER ADVERBS**
Mail <u>arrives</u> **regularly**.	an **extremely** <u>exciting</u> time	**most** <u>cleverly</u> presented
Doves <u>sing</u> **mournfully**.	a **hopelessly** <u>difficult</u> problem	**quite** <u>calmly</u> answered
I <u>responded</u> **immediately**.	an **unusually** <u>sound</u> approach	declined **quite** <u>dramatically</u>

▶ Adjective or Adverb?

Sometimes, writers mistakenly use adjectives in the place of adverbs. This is illustrated in the following sentences. The italicized words are adjectives incorrectly used in place of adverbs. The adverb form follows the sentence.

Megan can think of answers very *quick*. [**quickly**]
Store these antiques very *careful*. [**carefully**]
Ernie whispered the news as *quiet* as he could. [**quietly**]

Take special care to choose the correct word when using verbs that deal with the senses: *feel, taste, look, smell, sound*. If the word following the verb describes a noun or pronoun that comes before the verb, use an adjective. On the other hand, if the word following the verb describes the verb, use an adverb. In the following table, the adjectives and adverbs are highlighted and the nouns or verbs they modify are underlined.

MODIFIERS WITH "SENSE" VERBS	
ADJECTIVES	**ADVERBS**
The entire <u>group</u> felt **sick** after lunch.	The massage therapist <u>felt</u> **gently** along the patient's spine.
The new <u>keyboard</u> looked **strange** to me.	The detective <u>looked</u> **carefully** at the evidence gathered by the pathologist.
The <u>explanation</u> sounded **plausible** to us.	The biologist <u>smelled</u> the container **gingerly**.

Good and Well

Good is an adjective. *Well* is an adverb. Sometimes, *good* is mistakenly used to describe a verb. Use *well* to describe an action. The words modified by *good* and *well* are underlined in these examples.

Brenton <u>did</u> **well** on the test.
<u>Raul</u> felt **good** after the marathon.
The new marketing strategy was **well** <u>planned</u>.
The <u>lasagna</u> smelled **good** when I walked through the door.

► Comparisons

Adjectives and adverbs change form when they are used in comparisons. When you compare two items, use the *comparative* form of the modifier. If you are comparing more than two items, use the *superlative* form of the modifier.

The comparative form is created in one of two ways:

1. Add *–er* to the modifier if it is a short word of one or two syllables.
2. Place the word *more* or the word *less* before the modifier if it is a multisyllable word.

In addition, some modifiers change form completely. Examine the samples in the following table. The first six lines of the table illustrate these special modifiers that change form. The rest use the two rules above.

MODIFIERS IN COMPARISONS		
MODIFIER	**COMPARATIVE (FOR TWO ITEMS)**	**SUPERLATIVE (MORE THAN TWO)**
good	better	best
well	better	best
many	more	most
much	more	most
bad	worse	worst
little	less or lesser	least
neat	neater	neatest
lovely	lovelier	loveliest
funny	funnier	funniest
extreme	more [or less] extreme	most [or least] extreme
intelligent	more [or less] intelligent	most [or least] intelligent
precisely	more [or less] precisely	most [or least] precisely

When comparing items in a prepositional phrase, use *between* for two items and *among* for three or more. Look at how the comparative and superlative forms are used in the following sentences.

Up is the **better** direction for the stock market to be going. [comparing two directions]
Blue looks **better** than any other color we've seen. [comparing two colors many times]
The Buick Park Avenue is the **best** luxury car available. [comparing more than two cars]
The Mississippi is the **best** river for walleye fishing. [comparing more than two rivers]
The first run model was **more thoroughly** tested than the prototype. [comparing two things]

Avoid Illogical or Unclear Comparisons

"Ellie is more disorganized than any woman" is an illogical statement. It implies that Ellie, who is a woman, is more disorganized than herself. Always include the words *other* or *else* to keep your comparisons from being illogical.

> Ellie is more disorganized than any **other** woman.
> Ted can concentrate better than anyone **else** in our division.

Avoid Double Comparisons

A double comparison occurs when a writer uses both *–er* or *–est* and *more* or *most*. The following table provides examples of common mistakes and how to correct them.

DOUBLE COMPARISONS	
WRONG	**CORRECT**
Diane is the most friendliest person I know.	Diane is the friendliest person I know.
Judi is less sleepier than I am.	Judi is less sleepy than I am.
The writing in this sample seems more plainer than the writing in the other sample.	The writing in this sample seems plainer than the writing in the other sample.

Avoid Double Negatives

When a negative word is added to a statement that is already negative, a double negative results. Avoid double negatives in your writing. The words *hardly* and *barely* can cause problems; they function as negative words. In the following example sentences, the negative words are highlighted. Pay close attention to how the incorrect sentences are rewritten to avoid the double negative.

DOUBLE NEGATIVES	
WRONG	**CORRECT**
The warehouse **doesn't** have **no** surplus stock at this time.	The warehouse has **no** surplus stock at this time. The warehouse **doesn't** have any surplus stock at this time.
I **can't hardly** understand this financial report.	I can **hardly** understand this financial report. I **can't** understand this financial report.
The cash on hand **won't barely** cover this expense.	The cash on hand will **barely** cover this expense. The cash on hand **won't** cover this expense.

▶ Misplaced and Dangling Modifiers

Misplaced Modifiers
Place words, phrases, or clauses that describe nouns and pronouns as closely as possible to the words they describe. Failure to do this often results in a misplaced modifier—and a sentence that means something other than what was intended.

Words
For example, the words *only, almost,* and *just* should be placed as closely as possible to the word described. The best place is right before the words they describe. The placement of the word affects the meaning of the sentence.

The customers **only** looked at two samples.
The customers looked at **only** two samples.

In the first sentence, the customers "only looked" at the samples; they didn't touch them. In the second sentence, the customers looked at "only two," not three or four, samples. The placement of *only* changes the meaning.

Here's an example with *almost:*

Chad **almost** scored three touchdowns.
Chad scored **almost** three touchdowns.

In the first version, Chad "almost scored" three times—he must have come close to the goal line three times without actually crossing. In the second version, Chad scored "almost three" touchdowns—maybe 2.2 touchdowns. How many points are awarded for that?

Here's how placing *just* can affect the meaning of a sentence:

The Hill family **just** leases a car.
The Hill family leases **just** a car.

In the first version, the Hill family "just leases" a car, so they don't own or buy a car. In the second, they lease "just a car," not a truck or a van or any other vehicle.

Phrases and Clauses
Phrases and clauses that describe nouns or pronouns must also be placed as closely as possible to the words they describe. The sentences in the table below contain misplaced modifiers. Pay close attention to how they are rewritten to clarify the meaning.

MISPLACED MODIFIERS	
WRONG	CORRECT
The veterinarian explained how to vaccinate hogs in the community center basement. [Why would you want hogs in the community center?]	In the community center basement, the veterinarian explained how to vaccinate hogs. The veterinarian in the community center basement explained how to vaccinate hogs.
A big dog followed the old man that was barking loudly. [Why was the man barking?]	A big dog that was barking loudly followed the old man. Barking loudly, a big dog followed the old man.

Dangling Modifiers

Words, phrases, or clauses that begin a sentence and are set off by commas sometimes mistakenly modify the wrong noun or pronoun. These are called *dangling modifiers*. The following sentences contain dangling modifiers. Pay close attention to how the sentences are rewritten to avoid the problem.

DANGLING MODIFIERS	
WRONG	**CORRECT**
Flat and useless, Jason removed the bicycle tire. [Why was Jason flat?]	Jason removed the flat and useless bicycle tire. Flat and useless, the bicycle tire was removed by Jason.
Attached to an old stump, Janette saw a No Fishing sign. [Why was Janette attached to an old stump?]	Janette saw a No Fishing sign attached to an old stump. The No Fishing sign attached to an old stump caught Janette's attention.
While cleaning up after dinner, the phone rang. [Don't you wish you had a phone that cleaned up after dinner?]	While I was cleaning up after dinner, the phone rang. While cleaning up after dinner, I heard the phone ring. The phone rang while I was cleaning up after dinner.

Practice

Circle the correct word in each of the following sentences. The answers to this set of questions can be found at the end of the lesson.

1. Leo walked home (quick, quickly).

2. Charlotte seemed (bored, boredly) during the long meeting.

3. The old door doesn't open as (easy, easily) as it used to.

4. My new laptop is more (portable, portably) than my old one.

5. If you ask (polite, politely), she is more likely to grant your request.

6. The customer at the end of the line looked (angry, angrily).

7. The residents assembled (slow, slowly) for the community meeting.

8. Our new sofa is more (comfortable, comfortably) than our old one.

9. Mr. Nash seemed (unhappy, unhappily) about the decision that was made.

10. Lisa looked (careful, carefully) for any errors in the report.

11. They searched (thorough, thoroughly) in the attic and the basement.

12. Franklin had (fewer, less) difficulty with the decision because he had (fewer, less) choices.

13. Josie is the (younger, youngest) of the twins and the (shorter, shortest) one in the whole family.

14. Macaroni and cheese tastes especially (good, well) if the ingredients are mixed (good, well).

15. The staff hasn't heard (anything, nothing) about the new vacation policy.

16. Divide these cookies (between, among) the two girls, but split the cake (between, among) all the guests at the party.

Choose the correctly written sentence from each of the following sets.

17. a. I like olives and pimentoes boiled in oil.
b. Boiled in oil, I like olives and pimentos.

18. a. While speeding along a country road, two deer dashed across the road in front of our car.
b. Two deer dashed across the road in front of our car as we were speeding along a country road.

19. a. At the age of four, my grandmother taught me to read.
b. When I was four, my grandmother taught me to read.

20. a. We heard about the bank robbers who were arrested on the evening news.
b. We heard on the evening news about the bank robbers who were arrested.

▶ **Answers**

1. quickly
2. bored
3. easily
4. portable
5. politely
6. angry
7. slowly
8. comfortable
9. unhappy
10. carefully
11. thoroughly
12. less, fewer
13. younger, shortest
14. good, well
15. anything
16. between, among
17. a.
18. b.
19. b.
20. b.

Skill Building until Next Time

Practice what you have learned in this lesson by listening to others speak. Many people make mistakes with modifiers as they speak. When you hear such a mistake, think about how you might rephrase what the person said to make it correct. Once again, don't feel compelled to correct the mistakes; just use them as opportunities for mental practice so that no one will have the opportunity to correct *you*.

16 ▶ Easily Confused Word Pairs

LESSON SUMMARY

Threw or *through*? *To, two,* or *too*? *Brake* or *break*? This lesson and the next review a host of words that are often confused with other words and show you when to use them.

T his lesson covers some of the most commonly confused word pairs, those you are likely to use in your writing. If you learn to distinguish these words, you can avoid errors in your writing. These words are divided into three separate sections with practice exercises at the end of each section. The italicized words following some of the entries are *synonyms*, words that can be substituted in a sentence for the easily confused words.

▶ Three-Way Confusion

Lead/Led/Lead

- **Lead** as a verb means *guide, direct.* As a noun, it means *front position.* It rhymes with *seed.*
- **Led** is a verb, the past tense of **lead**, meaning *guided, directed.* It rhymes with *red.*
- **Lead** is a noun that is *the name of a metal.* It rhymes with *red.*
  Examples:
  Geronimo **led** (*guided*) the small band to safety.
  We hope the next elected officials will **lead** (*guide*) us to economic recovery.

A pound of styrofoam weighs as much as a pound of **lead** (*the metal*).

Jake took the **lead** (*front position*) as the group headed out of town.

Quite/Quit/Quiet

- **Quite** is an adverb meaning *completely, very, entirely*. It rhymes with *fight*.
- **Quit** is a verb meaning *stop, cease* or *stopped, ceased*. It rhymes with *sit*.
- **Quiet** as an adjective means *calm, silent, noiseless*. As a verb, it means *soothe, calm*. As a noun, it means *tranquility, peacefulness*. It almost rhymes with *riot*.
  Example:
  The firm was **quite** (*very*) surprised when its most productive investment specialist **quit** (*stopped*) work and opted for the **quiet** (*calm*) life of a monk.

Right/Write/Rite

- **Right** is an adjective meaning *correct, proper, opposite of left*.
- **Write** is a verb meaning *record, inscribe*.
- **Rite** is a noun meaning *ceremony, ritual*.
  Example:
  I will **write** (*record*) the exact procedures so you will be able to perform the **rite** (*ceremony*) in the **right** (*proper*) way.

Sent/Cent/Scent

- **Sent** is a verb, the past tense of *send*. It means *dispatched, transmitted*.
- **Cent** is a noun meaning *one penny*, a coin worth .01 of a dollar.
- **Scent** is a noun meaning *odor, smell*.
  Example:
  For a mere **cent** (*penny*), I bought an envelope perfumed with the **scent** (*odor*) of jasmine, which I **sent** (*dispatched*) to my grandmother.

Sight/Site/Cite

- **Sight** as a noun means *ability to see*. As a verb, it means *see, spot*.
- **Site** is a noun meaning *location, position*.
- **Cite** is a verb meaning *quote, make reference to*.
  Examples:
  At ninety-five, my grandmother's **sight** (*ability to see*) was acute enough to **sight** (*spot*) even the smallest error in a crocheted doily.
  This is the proposed **site** (*location*) for the new building.
  You must **cite** (*make reference to*) the source of your information.

To/Too/Two

- **To** is a preposition or part of an infinitive. Use it only to introduce a prepositional phrase, which usually answers the question *where*, or before a verb. Use **to** for introducing a prepositional phrase: *to the store, to the top, to my home, to our garden, to his laboratory, to his castle, to our advantage, to an open door, to a song, to the science room*, etc. Use **to** as an infinitive (*to* followed by a verb, sometimes separated by adverbs): *to run, to jump, to want badly, to seek, to propose, to write, to explode, to sorely need, to badly botch, to carefully examine*, etc.
- **Too** is an adverb meaning *also, very*.
- **Two** is an adjective, *the name of a number*, as in one, two, three.
  Example:
  The couple went **to** (*preposition*) the deli **to** (*infinitive*) pick up **two** (*the number*) plate dinners because both of them were **too** (*very*) tired **to** (*infinitive*) cook dinner.

Where/Wear/Were

- **Where** is an adverb referring to *place, location*.
- **Wear** as a verb means *put on, tire*. As a noun, it means *deterioration*.
- **Were** is a verb, the plural past tense of *be*.

Examples:

The slacks **were** (*form of be*) too tight.

The tires showed excessive **wear** (*deterioration*).

They will **wear** (*tire*) out these shoes if they **wear** (*put on*) them too much.

Where (*location*) are the clothes you **were** (*form of be*) planning to **wear** (*put on*) tomorrow?

Practice

Circle the correct word in the parentheses. Answers can be found at the end of the lesson.

1. The (sent, cent, scent) of freshly baked bread filled the house.

2. In order for this package to be (sent, cent, scent), you must add another (sent, cent, scent) of postage.

3. When you (right, write, rite) the final report, please be sure you use the (right, write, rite) statistics.

4. The (right, write, rite) of baptism will be performed at Sunday's service.

5. If you (quite, quit, quiet) talking for a minute and give us some (quite, quit, quiet), I will be (quite, quit, quiet) happy to ask the others to maintain this (quite, quit, quiet) atmosphere for the duration of the meeting.

6. Will (lead, led) the team in scoring.

7. The health inspector will (lead, led) the effort to educate citizens about the dangers of paint chips that might contain (lead, led).

8. The researcher asked permission to (sight, site, cite) my study in his report.

9. From the top floor, we were able to (sight, site, cite) the (sight, site, cite) that was chosen for the new office building.

10. (Where, wear, were) did you vacation last summer?

11. The armchairs her grandmother gave her (where, wear, were) old, and they were definitely showing signs of (where, wear, were).

▶ Easy Misses

Brake/Break

- **Brake** as a verb means *slow, stop*. As a noun, it means *hindrance, drag*.
- **Break** as a verb means *separate, shatter, adjourn*. As a noun, it means *separation, crack, pause, opportunity*.

Examples:

During our **break** (*pause*), we spotted a **break** (*crack*) in the pipeline.

Brake (*slow*) gently when driving on glare ice by applying slight pressure to the **brake** (*drag*).

Passed/Past

- **Passed** is a verb, the past tense of *pass*, meaning *transferred, went ahead or by, elapsed, finished*.
- **Past** as a noun means *history*. As an adjective, it means *former*.

Examples:

The first runner **passed** (*transferred*) the baton to the second just as she **passed** (*went by*) the stands. Three seconds **passed** (*elapsed*) before the next runner came by.

Harriet **passed** (*finished*) her bar exam on the first try.

I must have been a dolphin in a **past** (*former*) life.

Avoid digging up the **past** (*history*) if you can.

Peace/Piece
- **Peace** is a noun meaning *tranquility*.
- **Piece** as a noun means *division, creation*. As a verb, it means *patch, repair*.
  Example:
  If you can **piece** (*patch*) together the **pieces** (*bits*) of this story, perhaps we can have some **peace** (*tranquility*) around here.

Plain/Plane
- **Plain** as an adjective means *ordinary, clear, simple*. As a noun, it refers to *flat country*, also sometimes written as **plains.**
- **Plane** is a noun meaning *airship* or *flat surface*. It is occasionally used as a verb or adjective meaning *level*.
  Examples:
  They wore **plain** (*ordinary*) clothes.
  It was **plain** (*clear*) to see.
  The meal we ate on the **plains** (*flat country*) was quite **plain** (*simple*).
  It was **plain** (*clear*) to us that the enemy did not see our **plane** (*airship*) sitting on the open **plain** (*flat country*).

Scene/Seen
- **Scene** is a noun meaning *view, site, commotion*.
- **Seen** is a verb, the past participle of *see*, meaning *observed, noticed*.
  Example:
  We caused quite a **scene** (*commotion*) at the **scene** (*site*) of the accident. It was the worst we had ever **seen** (*observed*).

Threw/Through
- **Threw** is a verb, the past tense of *throw*, meaning *tossed*.
- **Through** is an adverb or a preposition meaning *in one side and out the other*. Use **through** to introduce a prepositional phrase: *through the door, through the lobby, though the mist*.

Example:
Fred **threw** (*tossed*) the ball **through** (*in one side and out the other*) the hoop.

Weak/Week
- **Weak** is an adjective meaning *flimsy, frail*, and *powerless*.
- **Week** is a noun meaning *a period of seven days*.
  Example:
  The patient's heartbeat was so **weak** (*frail*) that the doctor was certain he would be dead within a **week** (*seven days*).

Which/Witch
- **Which** is a pronoun dealing with *choice*. As an adverb, it introduces a subordinate clause.
- **Witch** is a noun meaning *sorceress, enchantress*.
  Examples:
  Which (*choice*) one do you want?
  This car, **which** (*introduces subordinate clause*) I have never driven, is the one I'm thinking about buying.
  I don't know **which** (*choice*) **witch** (*enchantress*) I should consult about my future.

Practice
Circle the correct word in the parentheses. Answers can be found at the end of the lesson.

12. (Which, Witch) (which, witch) costume did you decide to wear to the party?

13. Mia (threw, through) the invitation in the trash as soon as she walked (threw, through) the door.

14. When she saw the biker ahead (brake, break), Sally slammed on her (brake, break) to avoid the (brake, break) in the concrete path.

15. Have you (scene, seen) the love (scene, seen) in the movie?

16. The confused (which, witch) didn't know (which, witch) ingredients to use in her potion.

17. Matthew's department has (passed, past) the record that was set by Kathy's department in the (passed, past) year.

18. Marlene was feeling (weak, week) after having the flu for a (weak, week).

19. It only took one (peace, piece) of good news to restore her (peace, piece) of mind.

20. The private (plain, plane) had a (plain, plane) tan interior.

▶ To Split or Not to Split

Already/All Ready
- **Already** is an adverb meaning *as early as this, previously, by this time.*
- **All ready** means *completely ready, totally ready.*
  Examples:
  > At age four, Brigitta is reading **already** (*as early as this*).
  > We had **already** (*previously, by this time*) finished.
  > Are we **all ready** (*completely ready*) to go?

Altogether/All Together
- **Altogether** is an adverb meaning *entirely, completely.*
- **All together** means *simultaneously.*
  Examples:
  > These claims are **altogether** (*entirely*) false.
  > The audience responded **all together** (*simultaneously*).

Everyday/Every Day
- **Everyday** is an adjective meaning *ordinary, usual.*
- **Every day** means *each day.*

Examples:
> These are our **everyday** (*usual*) low prices.
> The associates sort the merchandise **every day** (*each day*).

Maybe/May Be
- **Maybe** is an adverb meaning *perhaps.*
- **May be** is a verb phrase meaning *might be.*
  Example:
  > **Maybe** (*perhaps*) the next batch will be better than this one. On the other hand, it **may be** (*might be*) worse.

Always Split
- **A lot.** There's no such word as *alot.* There's a word *allot*, but it means *to portion out* something.
  Example:
  > I thought it was all right that we **allotted** tickets to **a lot** of our best customers.

Practice
Circle the correct word in the parentheses.

21. I (where, wear, were) my (everyday, every day) clothes almost (everyday, every day).

22. (Maybe, may be) we should design a new model. It (maybe, may be) just the thing to brighten our financial picture.

23. If you had been (already, all ready), we could have (already, all ready) begun.

24. You'll be (alright, all right) if you follow the instructions.

25. When the staff is (altogether, all together), we should have (altogether, all together) enough brainpower for this project.

► Answers

1. scent
2. sent, cent
3. write, right
4. rite
5. quit, quiet, quite, quiet
6. led
7. lead, lead
8. cite
9. sight, site
10. Where
11. were, wear
12. Which, witch
13. threw, through

14. brake, brake, break
15. seen, scene
16. witch, which
17. passed, past
18. weak, week
19. piece, peace
20. plane, plain
21. wear, everyday, every day
22. Maybe, may be
23. all ready, already
24. all right
25. all together, altogether

Skill Building until Next Time

How many easily confused words can you spot in your reading? Try substituting the synonyms you learned.

More Easily Confused Words

LESSON SUMMARY
Some of the most commonly used words in the English language are easily confused with other equally common words. To avoid confusing readers, you need to know which ones are which.

This lesson covers more of the most commonly confused word pairs, those you are likely to use in your writing. If you learn to distinguish these words, you can avoid errors. The words are divided into three separate sections with practice exercises at the end of each section. The words in italics following some of the entries are *synonyms*, words that can be substituted in a sentence for the easily confused words.

▶ Small but Tricky

By/Buy
- **By** is a preposition used to introduce a phrase (by the book, by the time, by the way)
- **Buy** as a verb means *purchase*. As a noun, it means *bargain, deal*.
  Examples:
    We stopped **by** *(preposition)* the store to **buy** *(purchase)* some groceries.
    That car was a great **buy** (deal).

Dear/Deer

- **Dear** is an adjective meaning *valued, loved*.
- **Deer** is a noun referring to an *animal*, a four-legged one that lives in the woods and looks like Bambi.

  Example:

  My **dear** *(loved)* daughter's favorite movie is *Bambi*, about a **deer** *(animal)*.

Die/Dye

- **Die** is a verb meaning *pass away, fade*.
- **Dye** as a verb means to *color, tint*. As a noun, it refers to *coloring, pigment*.

  Example:

  We waited for the wind to **die** *(fade)* before we decided to **dye** *(color)* the sheets.

Hear/Here

- **Hear** is a verb meaning *listen to*.
- **Here** is an adverb meaning *in this place, to this place*.

  Example:

  Please come **here** *(to this place)* so you can **hear** *(listen to)* what I have to say.

Hole/Whole

- **Hole** is a noun meaning *opening, gap*.
- **Whole** as an adjective means *entire, intact*. As a noun, it means *entire part or amount*.

  Examples:

  The **whole** *(entire)* group heard the message. They patched the **hole** *(opening)* in the wall.

Knew/New

- **Knew** is a verb, the past tense of *know*. It means *understood, recognized*.
- **New** is an adjective meaning *fresh, different, current*.

  Example:

  I **knew** *(understood)* they were planning to buy a **new** *(different)* car.

Know/No

- **Know** is a verb meaning *understand, recognize*.
- **No** as an adverb means *not so, not at all*. As an adjective, it means *none, not one*.

  Example:

  As far as I **know** *(understand)*, we have **no** *(not one)* more of these shoes in stock.

Meat/Meet

- **Meat** is a noun meaning *food, flesh, main part*.
- **Meet** as a verb means *assemble, greet, fulfill*. As a noun, it means *assembly*.

  Examples:

  Before a track **meet** *(assembly)*, it is better to eat foods high in carbohydrates rather than **meat** *(flesh)*.

  The **meat** *(main part)* of his message was that our efforts did not **meet** *(fulfill)* his standards.

One/Won

- **One** can be an adjective meaning *single*. It can also be a pronoun used to mean a single person or thing.
- **Won** is a verb, the past tense of *win*. It means *prevailed, achieved, acquired*.

  Example:

  Jacquez is the **one** *(pronoun referring to Jacquez)* who **won** *(achieved)* the most improved bowler trophy this year.

Seam/Seem

- **Seam** is a noun meaning *joint, joining point*.
- **Seem** is a verb meaning *appear*.

  Example:

  Does it **seem** *(appear)* to you as if this **seam** *(joint)* is weakening?

Practice

Circle the correct word in the parentheses. Answers can be found at the end of the lesson.

1. If you don't get to the theater (by, buy) noon, there will not be any tickets left to (by, buy).

2. The best (by, buy) in the store is that new book written (by, buy) the famous talk show host. You should (by, buy) it.

3. The painting of the (dear, deer) that hung on the living room wall was quite (dear, deer) to our mother.

4. If you want to change the color of that shirt, you can (die, dye) it.

5. The rose bush started to (die, dye) soon after we planted it.

6. I can (hear, here) the speaker much better now that I am sitting (hear, here).

7. The (hole, whole) flood began by water leaking through a (hole, whole) in the pipe.

8. My wife (knew, new) everything about the (knew, new) digital camera.

9. I didn't (know, no) that that you had (know, no) idea how to get to the restaurant.

10. We asked to (meat, meet) the chef so we could tell her how much we enjoyed the (meat, meet) dish we ordered.

11. The undefeated varsity baseball team (one, won) the game by only (one, won) point.

12. I (seam, seem) to remember that the tailor did a flawless job repairing the (seam, seem) on my coat.

▶ Often Used and Misused

Choose/Chose

- **Choose** is a verb meaning *select*. It rhymes with *bruise*.
- **Chose** is past tense of *choose*; it means *selected*. It rhymes with *hose*.
  Example:
  > Henry **chose** (*selected*) flex hours on Friday afternoons. I will **choose** (*select*) the same option.

Loose/Lose/Loss

- **Loose** is an adjective meaning *free, unrestrained, not tight*. It rhymes with *goose*.
- **Lose** is a verb meaning *misplace, to be defeated, fail to keep*. It rhymes with *shoes*.
- **Loss** is a noun meaning *defeat, downturn, the opposite of victory or gain*. It rhymes with *toss*.
  Examples:
  > The chickens ran **loose** (*free*) in the yard.
  > The knot holding the boat to the dock was **loose** (*not tight*).
  > Where did you **lose** (*misplace*) your gloves?
  > The investors will **lose** (*fail to keep*) considerable capital if the market suffers a **loss** (*downturn*).

Suppose/Supposed

- **Suppose** is a verb meaning *assume, imagine*.
- **Supposed** as a verb is the past tense of *suppose* and means *assumed, imagined*. As an adjective, it means *expected, obligated*.
  Examples:
  > I **suppose** (*assume*) you'll be late, as usual.
  > We all **supposed** (*assumed*) you would be late.
  > You were **supposed** (*expected*) to have picked up the copies of the report before you came to the meeting.

Than/Then

- **Than** is a conjunctive word used to make a comparison.
- **Then** is an adverb telling *when* or meaning *next*.

Example:

> **Then** *(next),* the group discussed the ways in which the new procedures worked better **than** *(conjunction making a comparison)* the old.

Use/Used

- **Use** as a verb means *utilize, deplete.* It rhymes with *ooze.* As a noun, it rhymes with *goose* and means *purpose.*
- **Used** as a verb is the past tense of *use* and means *utilized, depleted.* As an adjective, it means *secondhand.*
- **Used to** can be used as an adjective, meaning *accustomed to,* or as an adverb meaning *formerly.* (Note that you never write *use to* when you mean *accustomed to* or *formerly.*)

Examples:

> Just **use** *(utilize)* the same password we **used** *(utilized)* yesterday.
>
> What's the **use** *(purpose)* in trying yet another time?
>
> We should consider buying **used** *(secondhand)* equipment.
>
> We **used to** *(formerly)* require a second opinion.
>
> Residents of Buffalo, New York, are **used to** *(accustomed to)* cold temperatures.

Weather/Whether

- **Weather** is a noun referring to the *condition outside.*
- **Whether** is an adverb used when referring to *a possibility.*

Examples:

> The **weather** *(condition outside)* took a turn for the worse.
>
> Let me know **whether** *(a possibility)* you are interested in this new system.

Practice

Circle the correct word in the parentheses. The answers can be found at the end of the lesson.

13. Ms. Wallace interviewed each candidate twice to (choose, chose) the best person for the job.

14. She (choose, chose) that university because of its excellent business school.

15. After the (loose, lose, loss) of her job, she began to (loose, lose, loss) confidence.

16. The shoes she ordered from the catalogue were too (loose, lose, loss).

17. I knew that I would (loose, lose, loss) my temper if he came to work late again.

18. I (suppose, supposed) that the manager was (suppose, supposed) to tell the staff about the reorganization plans.

19. I waited until I'd collected more (then, than) enough donations and (then, than) I contacted the director of the homeless shelter.

20. We (use, used) to buy (use, used) records whenever we went to thrift stores, but now we have no (use, used) for them.

21. You are (suppose, supposed) to enjoy your vacation (weather, whether) or not the (weather, whether) is beautiful.

▶ Killer *a*'s and *al*'s

Accept/Except/Expect

- **Accept** is a verb meaning *receive, bear.*
- **Except** is a preposition meaning *but, excluding.*
- **Expect** is a verb meaning *anticipate, demand, assume.*

    Examples:

    This client **expects** *(demands)* nothing **except** *(but)* the most sophisticated options available.

    Will you **accept** *(bear)* the responsibility for this decision?

    We **expect** *(anticipate)* everyone to come **except** *(excluding)* John.

Advice/Advise

- **Advice** is a noun meaning *suggestion, suggestions.* It rhymes with *ice.* (Hint: Think *advICE.*)
- **Advise** is a verb meaning *suggest to, warn.* It rhymes with *wise.*

    Examples:

    We **advise** *(suggest to)* you to proceed carefully.

    That was the best **advice** *(suggestion)* I've received so far.

Affect/Effect

- **Affect** is a verb meaning *alter, inspire* or *move emotionally, imitate.* **Affected**, besides being the past tense of *affect*, can also be used as an adjective meaning *imitated, pretentious.*
- **Effect** as a noun means *consequence.* As a verb, it means *cause.*

    Examples:

    How will this plan **affect** *(alter)* our jobs? What **effect** *(consequence)* will this restructuring have on profits? Will it **effect** *(cause)* an increase?

    The movie **affected** *(moved emotionally)* Marian.

    He **affected** *(imitated)* an English accent.

    The **affected** *(pretentious)* speech fooled no one.

Capital/Capitol

- **Capital** as a noun means either *assets* or *the city that is the seat of government.* As an adjective, it means *main, very important,* or *deserving of death.*
- **Capitol** is a noun referring to *the building that houses the government.*

    Examples:

    How much **capital** *(assets)* are you willing to invest?

    I think that's a **capital** *(main)* objective.

    First-degree murder is a **capital** *(deserving of death)* crime.

    Albany is the **capital** *(city)* of New York.

    No legislators were injured in the explosion in the **capitol** *(building).*

Personal/Personnel

- **Personal** is an adjective meaning *private.*
- **Personnel** as a noun means *staff, employees* or as an adjective means *dealing with staff or employees.*

    Example:

    The director of **personnel** *(staff)* keeps all the **personnel** *(employee)* files in order and guards any **personal** *(private)* information they contain.

Principal/Principle

- **Principal** as a noun refers to the *head of a school* or an *investment.* As an adjective, it means *primary, major.*
- **Principle** is a noun meaning *rule, law, belief.*

    Examples:

    The **principal** *(head)* of Calbert High School used the **principal** *(investment)* of an endowment fund to cover this month's salaries.

    The **principal** *(primary)* objective is to make decisions that are in keeping with our **principles** *(beliefs).*

Practice

Circle the correct word in the parentheses. The answers can be found at the end of the lesson.

22. Surely you didn't (accept, except, expect) Weldon to (accept, except, expect) responsibility for this decision when everyone (accept, except, expect) him was consulted.

23. We (accept, except, expect) the delivery to arrive early in the morning.

24. The soothsayer will (advice, advise) you to seek her (advice, advise) often.

25. The new work schedule (affected, effected) production in a positive way.

26. How will this new work schedule (affect, effect) production?

27. What (affect, effect) will this new work schedule have on production?

28. We plan to tour the (capital, capitol) building whenever we visit a state's (capital, capitol) city.

29. We never release (personal, personnel) information about our (personal, personnel).

30. The employees' (principal, principle) concern is workload.

31. The new legislation violates the basic (principals, principles) upon which the country was founded.

▶ Answers

1. by, buy
2. buy, by, buy
3. deer, dear
4. dye
5. die
6. hear, here
7. whole, hole
8. knew, new
9. know, no
10. meet, meat
11. won, one
12. seem, seam
13. choose
14. chose
15. loss, lose
16. loose
17. lose
18. suppose, supposed
19. than, then
20. used, used, use
21. supposed, whether, weather
22. expect, accept, except
23. expect
24. advise, advice
25. affected
26. affect
27. effect
28. capitol, capital
29. personal, personnel
30. principal
31. principles

Skill Building until Next Time

Make a conscious effort to use the correct forms of these easily confused words in your writing. You may find it helpful to copy the words and their synonyms onto a separate sheet of paper. This will provide a good review and serve as a handy reference you can keep with you as you write.

LESSON

18▶ Diction

LESSON SUMMARY

"Diction?" you might think. "In a book about writing?" While *diction* refers to how words are pronounced, it also refers to *which* words you choose. To use language effectively, writers have to write concisely and precisely. This lesson and Lesson 19 focus on how to choose the words that best communicate what you want to say.

word is a terrible thing to waste. Or is it better to say, "It is a terrible thing to waste a word"? The difference between these two versions is a matter of *diction*, using appropriate words and combining them in the right way to communicate your message accurately. This lesson discusses ways to avoid some of the most common diction traps: wordiness, lack of precison, clichés, and jargon. Learning to recognize and avoid such writing weaknesses will turn a mediocre writer into a good one—this means expressing ideas in the *best* and *clearest* possible way.

▶ Wordiness

Excess words in communication waste space and time. Not only that, but they may also distort the message or make it difficult for the reader to understand. Get in the habit of streamlining your writing, making the sentences as concise as possible. If you use five words where three would do, delete the extra words or structure your sentences to avoid them. See if you can rewrite the sentences in the first column to make them less wordy. Check yourself against the version in the second column.

The additional words in the first column add no information. All they do is take up space.

WORDY	REVISED
It was a three-hour period after the accident when the rescue squad that we knew was going to help us arrived. [21 words]	The rescue squad arrived three hours after the accident. [9 words]
It was decided that the church would organize a committee for the purpose of conducting a search for a new pastor. [21 words]	The church organized a committee to search for a new pastor. [11 words]

Buzzwords and Fluffy Modifiers

Buzzwords—such as *aspect, element, factor, scope, situation, type, kind, forms,* and so on—sound important, but add no meaning to a sentence. They often signal a writer who has little or nothing to say, yet wishes to sound important. Likewise, modifiers such as *absolutely, definitely, really, very, important, significant, current, major,* and *quite* may add length to a sentence, but they seldom add meaning.

Wordy:

The *nature of the* scheduling system is a *very important matter* that can *definitely* have a *really significant* impact on the morale *aspect* of an employee's attitude. *Aspects of* our current scheduling policy make it *absolutely necessary* that we undergo a *significant* change.

Revised:

The scheduling system can affect employee morale. Our policy needs to be changed.

The following table lists a host of phrases that can be reduced to one or two words.

WORDY	CONCISE	WORDY	CONCISE
puzzling in nature	puzzling	at this point in time	now; today
of a peculiar kind	peculiar	at that point in time	then
regardless of the fact that	although	in order to	to
due to the fact that	because	by means of	by
of an indefinite nature	indefinite	exhibits a tendency to	tends to
concerning the matter of	about	in connection with	with
in the event that	if	in relation to	with

Passive Voice

Some wordiness is caused by using passive voice verbs when you could use the active voice. (See Lesson 11 if you don't remember passive voice.)

PASSIVE	ACTIVE
It has been decided that your application for grant money is not in accordance with the constraints outlined by the committee in the application guidelines.	The committee denied your grant because it did not follow the application guidelines.
The letter of resignation was accepted by the Board of Directors.	The Board of Directors accepted the resignation.

Intellectual-ese

Those passive sentences suffer not only from passive voice wordiness, but also from the writer's attempt to make the writing sound intellectual, to make the message more difficult than necessary. Writers make this error in many ways. One way is to turn adjectives and verbs into nouns. This transformation usually means extra words are added to sentence.

WORDY	REVISED
Water *pollution* [noun] is not as serious in the northern parts of Canada.	Water is not as *polluted* [adjective] in northern Canada.
Customer *demand* [noun] is reducing in the area of sales services.	Customers *demand* [verb] fewer sales services.

Another way writers add words without adding meaning is to use a pretentious tone. What follows is an actual memo issued by a bureaucrat during World War II. When it was sent to President Franklin Roosevelt for his approval, he edited the memo before sending it on.

Original pretentious memo:
In the unlikely event of an attack by an invader of a foreign nature, such preparations shall be made as will completely obscure all Federal buildings and non-Federal buildings occupied by the Federal government during an air raid for any period of time from visibility by reason of internal or external illumination.

Roosevelt's revised memo:
If there is an air raid, put something across the windows and turn off the lights outside in buildings where we have to keep the work going.

Here's another example of pretentious writing, along with a clearer, revised version.

Pompous memo:
As per the most recent directive issued from this office, it is incumbent upon all employees and they are henceforth instructed to reduce in amount the paper used in the accomplishment of their daily tasks due to the marked increase in the cost of such supplies.

Revised:
Since paper costs have increased, employees must use less paper.

WORD ECONOMY	
STRETCHED SENTENCE	**CONCISE SENTENCE**
Cassandra seems to be content.	Cassandra seems content.
We must know what it is that we are doing.	We must know what we're doing.
This is the book of which I have been speaking.	I spoke about this book.
It is with pleasure that I announce the winner.	I am pleased to announce the winner.
The reason we were late was because of traffic.	We were late because of traffic.
These plans will be considered on an individual basis.	These plans will be considered individually.
The caterer, who was distressed, left the party.	The distressed caterer left the party.
There are new shipments arriving daily.	New shipments arrive daily.
Due to the fact that we were late, we missed the door prizes.	We came late and missed the door prizes.
The consideration given in the latest promotion is an example of how I was treated unfairly.	I was not fairly considered for the latest promotion.

Writers sometimes stretch their sentences with unnecessary words, all to sound intelligent. The previous table illustrates stretched sentences that have been rewritten more concisely.

Redundancy

Another writing trap that takes up space is *redundancy*, repeating words that express the same idea or in which the meanings overlap. If you stop to think about phrases like the following—and many others—you'll see that the extra words are not only unnecessary but often just plain silly.

enclosed *with this letter*
remit *payment*
absolutely necessary
weather *outside*
postpone *until later*
refer *back*
past history

ask *the question*
continue *on*, proceed *ahead*
repeated *over again*
gather *together*
compulsory requirement
temporarily suspended
necessary requirements
plain *and simple*

Enclosed means it's in this letter, doesn't it? *Remit* means *pay*. And how can something be more *necessary* than *necessary*? The weather *outside* as opposed to the weather *inside*? *Past* history as opposed to . . . ? You see the point. Keep it simple. (Not *plain and simple.*)

Practice

Try rewriting the following sentences to remove the fluffy wording. Suggested revisions are at the end of this lesson, but your versions may be different; there's more than one way to rewrite these sentences.

1. Stephanie is a very important employee who has played a significant role in the success of this company.

2. Some educators hold with the opinion that corporal punishment should in fact be reinstated in our schools to act as a deterrent to those students who are considering engaging in inappropriate behavior.

3. It is certainly a true statement that bears repeating over and over again that technological advancements such as computers can assist employees in performing in a very efficient manner, and that these self-same computers may in fact result in considerable savings over a period of time.

4. I arrived at a decision to allow the supervisor of my department to achieve a higher golf score in order to enhance my opportunities for advancement in the event that such opportunities became available.

▶ **Precise Language**

Make your writing as precise as possible. In doing so, you communicate more meaning using fewer words. In other words, you make your writing more concise. Choose exact verbs, modifiers, and nouns to help you transmit an exact meaning, such as the examples in the following table.

IMPRECISE VS. PRECISE	
VERBS	
Emilia participated in the protest.	Emilia organized the march on the capital.
Hannah won't deal with sales meetings.	Hannah won't attend sales meetings.
Dick can relate to Jane.	Dick understands Jane's feelings.
MODIFIERS	
These bad instructions confused me.	These disorganized, vague instructions left me with no idea how to repair the leak.
Toy Story is a good movie with fun for all.	*Toy Story* is a clever animated film with humor, adventure, and romance.
We had a nice time with you.	We enjoyed eating your food, drinking your cola, and swimming in your pool.
NOUNS	
I always have trouble with this computer.	I can never get this computer to save or print.
I like to have fun when I take a vacation.	I like to swim, fish, and eat out when I'm on vacation.
Let me grab some things from my locker.	Let me grab my purse and books from my locker.

Abstract vs. Concrete

Abstract language refers to intangible ideas or to classes of people and objects rather than the people or things themselves. Abstractions are built on concrete ideas. Without a grasp of the concrete meanings, a reader can't be expected to understand an abstract idea. Journalists and law enforcement professionals are especially aware of the distinction between abstract and concrete as they write. They strive to present the facts clearly, so the reader can draw conclusions. They avoid making the assumptions for the reader, hoping the facts will speak for themselves. Concrete language requires more time and thought to write, but it communicates a message more effectively. Additional words are an advantage if they add meaning or increase precision.

ABSTRACT ASSUMPTION	CONCRETE DETAILS
Strader was amazing.	Strader scored 28 points, grabbed 12 rebounds, and blocked 5 shots.
The couple was in love.	The couple held hands, hugged, and ignored everything around them.
Billie is reliable and responsible.	Billie always arrives on time, completes her assignments, and helps others if she has time.

Clichés

A *cliché* is a tired, overworked phrase that sucks the life out of writing. These are cliché phrases: *a needle in a haystack, quiet as a mouse, crack of dawn, tough as nails, naked truth, hear a pin drop,* and so on. Authors use clichés when they don't have the time or ability to come up with more precise or more meaningful language. Although clichés are a sort of "communication shorthand," they rely on stereotypical thinking for their meaning. A writer who uses clichés is relying on unoriginal, worn-out thinking patterns to carry a message. If the message is important, fresh language will make a stronger impression than old, overused phrases. Original language stimulates thought and heightens the reader's concentration. Moreover, a fresh image rewards an attentive reader.

Imagine that a writer wanted to explain how difficult it was to find the source of a problem. Look at the following two versions. One relies on a cliché to communicate the message; the other uses a fresher, more original approach. Which version is likely to make the stronger impression, to communicate the message more effectively?

Finding the source of this problem was harder than finding a needle in a haystack.
Finding the source of this problem was harder than finding a fact in a political advertisement.

Here are more examples contrasting clichés with fresher, more original language. When you check your writing, look for ways to replace frequently used words and phrases with something fresh and original.

We rose at the crack of dawn.
We rose with the roosters.

Having Sam at our negotiations meetings was like having a loose cannon on deck.
Having Sam at our negotiations meetings was like having a German shepherd's tail in your crystal closet.

Jargon

Jargon is the technical, wordy language used by those associated with a trade or profession. Often, it is full of passive voice, acronyms, technical terms, and abstract words. Writers use jargon to sound educated, sophisticated, or knowledgeable. Actually, jargon muddies and even distorts the message. Compare the following two paragraphs.

Alex demonstrates a tendency to engage inappropriately in verbal social interaction during class time. His grades are deficient because he suffers from an unwillingness to complete supplementary assignments between class periods.

Alex talks in class when he isn't supposed to. He has low grades because he doesn't do his homework.

The first paragraph leaves the impression that Alex is a sociopath with a serious problem. The second portrays him as a student who needs to talk less and work more. When you write, strive for clear, plain language that communicates your message accurately. Clear communication leaves a better impression by far than pretentious, abstract, jargon-filled words.

Practice

Choose the option that expresses the idea most clearly and concisely. Answers are at the end of the lesson.

5. a. On Thursday evening, our community garden club had a plant sale. The money raised will be used to replace the trees in Memorial Park that were lost in the storm.

  b. Some time late last week, the members of our community garden club organized and ran a plant sale to raise money. The money they collected at the sale is for the purpose of buying new trees to replace the ones that were lost in Memorial Park during the huge storm.

6. a. The least expensive option in a situation such as this is inevitably also the most advantageous option.

  b. The cheapest way is the best way.

7. a. Too many Americans prefer unhealthy, high-calorie fast food to healthy, natural options.

  b. Too many Americans prefer cheeseburgers and fries to steamed vegetables and rice.

8. a. The marketing department found that customers prefer the vanilla scent.

  b. Consumer attitude studies conducted by our marketing department seem to indicate that a large majority of our customers had good things to say about the vanilla scent.

▶ Answers

1. Stephanie has contributed a lot to this company's success.

2. Some educators believe that unruly students should be spanked.

3. Using computers can save time and money.

4. I let my supervisor beat me at golf so she would promote me.

5. a.

6. b.

7. b.

8. a.

Skill Building until Next Time

Listen to public officials as they deliver prepared speeches. Do they speak clearly and plainly, or are they trying to sound "official"? A truly competent, intelligent speaker or writer doesn't need a mask of pretentious, abstract, sophisticated-sounding language.

LESSON

19 ▶ More Diction

LESSON SUMMARY

This lesson continues the ideas presented in the last lesson: writing clearly and communicating accurately. It covers colloquialism, loaded language, consistent point of view, parallelism, and gender-neutral language.

Good writers know that communicating requires choosing words carefully. Writing styles that are too formal or informal, inappropriate, or just plain emotional turn readers off. You may have the best ideas in the world, but if you can't get them across in writing, no one will ever act on your great ideas. On the other hand, well-expressed, commonplace ideas are more likely to get attention. How you choose your words has everything to do with whether your writing gets the attention it deserves.

▶ Colloquialism

Colloquialisms are informal words and phrases such as *a lot, in a bind, pulled it off,* and so on. These words and phrases are widely used in conversations between friends, but in written communication, they portray an attitude of chumminess or close friendship that may cause your message to be taken less seriously than you intended. You may even insult your reader without meaning to. A friendly, colloquial tone is fine in a personal letter; however, a more formal tone is better for business communications, which are meant to be taken seriously. Compare the following paragraphs. If you received these two memos from an employee, which would you take more seriously?

> I think the way we promote people around here stinks. People who aren't that good at their jobs get promoted just because they pal around with the right people. That puts across the idea that it doesn't matter how much time I put in at work or how good of a job I do; I won't get promoted unless I kiss up to the boss. I'm not that kind of guy.

> I think our promotion system is unfair. Average and below-average employees receive promotions simply because they befriend their superiors. This practice leaves the impression that commitment and quality of work are not considered. I choose not to socialize with my supervisors, and I feel as though I am not being promoted for that reason alone.

The writer of the first paragraph sounds as if he doesn't take his job all that seriously. And yet he probably does; he just hasn't managed to communicate his seriousness in writing because he has used language that is more appropriate in a conversation with his friends than a memo to his supervisor. The writer of the second paragraph, on the other hand, conveys his seriousness by using more formal language. He has done so without falling into the opposite trap, discussed in the last lesson, of trying to sound *too* intelligent. He has used plain, but not colloquial, language.

The sentences at the bottom of the page illustrate the difference between colloquial and formal diction. By substituting the highlighted words, the sentence becomes more formal rather than colloquial.

▶ Tone

Tone describes a writer's emotional attitude toward the subject or the audience. The more reasonable and objective a message seems, the more likely it is to be considered seriously. Raging emotions seldom convince anyone to change an opinion, and they seldom convince anyone who is undecided. Persuasion requires clearly presented facts and logically presented arguments. A reader or listener will give the most credibility to an argument that seems fair and objective. Emotion can reduce credibility. Use it carefully.

Avoid Anger

Avoid accusatory, angry words that make demands. Consider the two paragraphs on the next page. Which one is most likely to persuade the reader to take action?

COLLOQUIAL	MORE FORMAL WORDS
I have around three hours to finish this task.	I have **about** three hours to finish this task.
The pasta was real good.	The pasta was **very** good.
We got sick from the food.	We **became ill** from the food.
It looks like we could win.	It looks **as if** we could win.
I'm awful tired.	I'm **very** (or **quite** or **extremely**) tired.

I just got this stupid credit card bill in the mail. None of these outrageous charges are mine. I can't believe some big corporation like yours can't find a way to keep its records straight or keep its customers from being cheated. If you can't do any better than that, why don't you just give it up? I reported my stolen credit card five days before any of these charges were made, and yet you idiots have charged me for these purchases. The fine print you guys are so fond of putting in all of your contracts says I am not (I'll say it again just to help you understand) **not** responsible for these charges. I want them removed immediately.

The credit card bill I received on April 25 contains several charges that need to be removed. I reported my stolen credit card on April 20. When I called to make the report, the representative referred me to the original contract that states, "No charges in excess of $50.00 nor any made more than 24 hours after the card has been reported stolen shall be charged to the customer's account." Naturally, I was quite relieved. All of the charges on this account were made more than 24 hours after I reported the stolen card. Please remove the charges from my account. Thank you very much.

No matter how angry you might be, giving your reader the benefit of the doubt is not only polite but also more likely to get results. (This principle is even more important when you're writing a supervisor, employee, or client than when you're writing a big credit card company.) The first letter is the one you might write in the heat of the moment when you first get your credit card bill. In fact, writing that letter might help you get the anger out of your system. Tearing it up will make you feel even better. *Then* you can sit down and write the letter you're actually going to send—the second version.

Use *sarcasm* (bitter, derisive language) and *irony* (saying the opposite of what you actually mean) carefully in your writing. Like anger, sarcasm brings your credibility into question. Overusing sarcasm can make you seem childish or petty rather than reasonable and logical. Furthermore, for irony to be successful, the reader must immediately recognize it. Unless the reader fully understands, you risk confusing or distorting your message. A little well-placed irony or sarcasm may invigorate your writing, but it requires careful, skillful use.

Avoid Cuteness

Avoid words that make your writing sound flippant, glib, or cute. Although the writing may be entertaining to the reader, it might not be taken seriously. The following paragraph protests a decision, but fails to offer a single reason why the decision was wrong. It may get the attention of the reader, but it won't produce any results, except perhaps the dismissal of its author.

I'm just a li'l ol' girl, but it's clear to me that this decision is dead wrong. I'm afraid that the people who made it have a serious intelligence problem. If they took their two IQ points and rubbed them together, they probably couldn't start gasoline on fire. If you were one of those people. . . . Oh well, it's been nice working for you.

The conclusion implied in this writer's last sentence—that she doesn't expect to work here much longer—is probably accurate.

Avoid Pompousness

Avoid words that make your writing sound pompous or preachy. Few people respond positively to a condescending, patronizing tone. Compare the two paragraphs on the next page, both written by employees seeking a promotion. Which employee would you promote if they were both vying for the same position and had nearly identical work records and qualifications?

If you examine my service and work record for the past two years, I believe you will find a dedicated, hardworking employee who is ideal for the floor manager position. I believe all employees should be on time for their jobs. You will see that my attendance record is impeccable, no absences and no tardies. You can see from my monthly evaluations that I was a high-quality employee when I was hired and that I have consistently maintained my high standards. I strive to be the kind of employee all managers wish to hire, and I believe my record shows this. I am also extremely responsible. Again, my record will reflect that my supervisors have confidence in me and assign additional responsibility readily to me because I am someone who can handle it. I am a man of my word, and believe that responsibility is something to be treasured, not shirked. As you compare me with other employees, I feel confident that you will find I am the most competent person available.

Thank you for considering me for the position of floor manager. As you make your decision, I would like to highlight three items from my service and work record. First, in two years, I have not missed work and have been tardy only once, as the result of an accident. Second, my supervisors have given me the highest ratings on each of the monthly evaluations. Finally, I was pleased to have been given additional responsibilities during my supervisors' vacation times, and I learned a great deal about managing sales and accounts as a result. I welcome the challenge that would come with a promotion. Thank you again for your consideration.

Both writers highlight the same aspects of their employment records. Yet the first writer seems so full of himself that his superiors might wonder whether he has the people skills to be an effective supervisor. No one wants to work for a supervisor who is prone to such pronouncements as "responsibility is something to be treasured, not shirked." The other writer's just-the-facts approach is bound to make a better impression on the decision-makers.

Avoid Cheap Emotion

Avoid language that is full of sentimentality or cheap emotion. You risk making your reader gag. The following paragraph illustrates this error.

> We were so deeply hurt by your cruel thoughtlessness in failing to introduce us to Jack Nicholson. He is the most wonderful, talented actor to have ever walked the face of the Earth. My friend Charlotte and I so admire him and have ever since we can remember. Our admiration is a deep-channeled river that will never stop flowing. I'm sure you can imagine just how sorely disappointed and deeply wounded we were when we were not given the opportunity and honor to shake the hand and hear the voice of this great man. Neither I nor my dearest friend can seem to forget this slight, and I'm sure we will remain scarred for many years to come.

Are you gagging yet? Instead of regretting not having introduced the writer to the great Jack Nicholson, the reader probably congratulates himself on not having let this nut case get near him.

▶ Consistent Point of View

Authors can write using the first-person point of view (*I, me, we, us, my, our*), second-person point of view (*you, your*), or third-person point of view (*she, he, one, they, her, him, them, hers, his, one's, theirs*). Avoid switching points of view within or between sentences. Keep the point of view consistent throughout.

INCONSISTENT	CONSISTENT
Citizens pay taxes, which entitles them [third person] to have some say in how their [third person] government is run. We [first person] have a right to insist on efficient use of our tax dollars.	We citizens pay taxes, which entitles us to have some say in how our government is run. We have a right to insist on efficient use of our tax dollars.
I [first person] enjoyed my trip to the park. You [second person] could see trees budding, flowers blooming, and baby animals running all over.	I enjoyed my trip to the park. I saw trees budding, flowers blooming, and baby animals running all over.

▶ Parallelism

Two or more equivalent ideas in a sentence that have the same purpose should be presented in the same form. This is called *parallel structure*. Using parallel sentence structures not only helps your writing flow smoothly, but also helps readers quickly recognize similar ideas. Look at the following examples of parallel words, phrases, and clauses.

NOT PARALLEL	PARALLEL
My roommate is miserly, sloppy, and a bore.	My roommate is miserly, sloppy, and boring. My roommate is a miser, a slob, and a bore.
My vacuum cleaner squealed loudly, shook violently, and dust filled the air.	My vacuum cleaner squealed loudly, shook violently, and filled the air with dust.
We soon discovered that our plane tickets were invalid, that our cruise reservations had never been made, and our travel agent left town.	We soon discovered that our plane tickets were invalid, that our cruise reservations had never been made, and that our travel agent had left town.

Pairs of ideas should always be presented in parallel constructions. The following sentences present two or more equivalent ideas using similar forms.

> The committee finds no original and inspiring ideas in your proposal. What is original is not inspiring, and what is inspiring is not original.
> We came, we saw, we conquered.
> Belle was a timid, talented, and creative person.
> Ask not what your country can do for you; ask what you can do for your country.

▶ Using Gender-Neutral Language

It may seem that language is neutral, simply a tool for expressing ideas. Although this is partly true, our language reflects our values and communicates to others our social biases about gender and other issues. If an entire culture is gender-biased, the language automatically becomes a vehicle for expressing and perpetuating those biases. One of the first steps toward overcoming such a prejudice is to examine the language and change it so that it no longer perpetuates false stereotypes about gender.

Some people resist changing the language, thinking that the words are harmless and that those who are offended are simply too sensitive. The fact remains that many readers are sensitive to, and offended by, the traditional use of masculine pronouns to refer to both sexes or by diminutive suffixes indicating gender. Saying, "Man must fulfill his destiny" or "Emily Dickinson was a great poetess" strikes them as archaic at best and insulting at worst.

Whenever emotionally charged words distract a reader, the message suffers. A reader who is offended by the words won't get the meaning.

Gender Traps

The following are samples of the type of language to avoid because the emotional charge may sidetrack the ideas.

Masculine Nouns or Pronouns

The most serious difficulty comes when using pronouns. If the pronoun *he* is used to refer to an indefinite person—a teacher, a student, a postal carrier—the underlying assumption seems to be that all teachers or students or postal carriers are male. The same problem comes up with words such as *someone, somebody, everyone, no one,* or *nobody.* Here are some examples of gender traps in sentences and possible ways to revise them.

POOR	BETTER
A presidential candidate must realize that his life is no longer his own.	Presidential candidates must realize that their lives are not their own
If a student wishes to change his schedule, he must see his advisor, who will tell him how to proceed.	a) If a student wishes to change his or her schedule, he or she must see his or her advisor, who will tell him or her how to proceed. [This sentence solves the mismatching number problem by using both a masculine and a feminine singular pronoun. However, the writing seems awkward and unwieldy.] b) If students wish to change their schedule, they must see their advisor, who will tell them how to proceed. [In this sentence, making the noun *student* into plural *students* solves the pronoun mismatch problem.] c) If you wish to change your schedule, see your advisor, who will tell you how to proceed. [This sentence uses the second-person pronouns "you" and "your."]
If anyone wants to improve his test scores, he should take good notes and study.	a) Anyone who wants improved test scores should take good notes and study. [Restructure the sentence to avoid the pronoun reference.] b) Students who want to improve their test scores should take good notes and study. [Turn *anyone* into the plural *students*.] c) Anyone who wants to improve his or her test scores should take good notes and study. [Use both the masculine and feminine singular pronouns.]

Note that you cannot simply change the words *he* and *his* to *they* and *theirs*. "If anyone wants to improve their test scores, they should good take notes and study" is grammatically incorrect. The pronouns *they* and *their* don't match their antecedent, anyone, in number, because *anyone* is singular and *they* is plural.

Women as Subordinate to Men
Writers can make it seem as if men are always leaders and women are always subordinate in many subtle ways.

POOR	BETTER
A principal and his staff need to establish good communication.	The principal and staff need to establish good communication.
If you ask the nurse, she will summon the doctor if he is available.	If you ask, a nurse will summon an available doctor.
Bob took his wife and children to a movie.	Bob and Mary took their children to a movie.
Emil asked his secretary to check the mail.	Emil asked the secretary to check the mail.

Writers also fall into a similar kind of trap when they refer to men according to their abilities, while referring to women according to their appearance.

POOR	BETTER
Dr. Routmeir and his attractive, blond wife arrived at the party at 9:00 P.M.	a) Dr. and Ms. Routmeir arrived at the party at 9:00 P.M. b) Herman and Betty Routmeir arrived at the party at 9:00 P.M.
The talented violinist and his beautiful accompanist took the stage.	The violinist and the accompanist took the stage.

Note that in both sentences in the first column, the man is referred to by his profession, while the woman is referred to by her appearance. To avoid the appearance of assigning value to men because of their accomplishments and to women because of their appearance, refer to both in the same context, either physical or professional. Furthermore, in the first example, the man is addressed by a formal title, and the woman is not identified except as the wife belonging to the man. To avoid the appearance of referring to the woman strictly as the possession of the man, refer to both by name.

"Men's" Jobs and "Women's" Jobs
Avoid making special note of gender when discussing a job traditionally done by men or women—those traditions don't hold anymore! The first sentence makes traditional assumptions, while the second does not.

When a man on board collapsed, a lady pilot emerged from the cockpit, and a male nurse offered assistance.
When a passenger collapsed, a pilot emerged from the cockpit, and a nurse offered assistance.

The references *lady pilot* and *male nurse* call attention to themselves because they assume that the reader will automatically assign a gender to the job. Readers who do not think in terms of the traditional stereotypes will be offended by the writer's assumption that they do engage in stereotypical thinking.

Avoiding Gender Traps

As a writer, you must understand the effect of gender references on readers. You can avoid offending readers unintentionally with gender-specific language in three ways: using gender-neutral terms, using the plural, or restructuring sentences altogether to avoid a gender reference. All these tactics have already been illustrated in the previous revised sentences. More examples appear next.

Use Gender-Neutral Terms

There are a lot of words in English that traditionally have taken different forms for male and female persons. These distinctions are becoming obsolete. Today, most people prefer one term to refer to both men and women in their particular roles. And this change doesn't have to be awkward, as you can see in the table at the bottom of the page.

In the past, it was common to use the word *man* to refer to all humanity, both men and women. Today, that usage will offend many readers. The following sentence demonstrates this kind of usage while the second one offers a more appropriate alternative.

> If man wishes to improve his environment, he must improve himself.
>
> If humanity wishes to improve its environment, each individual must improve.

Convert to the Plural

One of the stickiest gender-reference problems is how to deal with a sentence such as, "A student must do *his* homework if *he* wants to succeed in *his* classes." The easiest way to avoid those troublesome *he* words is to turn the singular pronouns *he, she, him, hers,* or *his* into the plural pronouns *they* and *their.* Of course, then you must also revise the antecedents of those pronouns so they are also plural (see Lesson 13): "*Students* must do *their* homework if *they* want to succeed in *their* classes." The table on the next page offers some other examples.

GENDER-SPECIFIC	GENDER-NEUTRAL
waiter, waitress	server
stewardess, steward	flight attendant
policeman, policewoman	police officer
chairwoman, chairman	chairperson, chair
man-made	synthetic, artificial
foreman	supervisor
manpower	employees, personnel
man, mankind	humanity, people

GENDER-SPECIFIC	GENDER-NEUTRAL
The doctor uses his best judgment.	Doctors use their best judgment.
Every student must do his homework.	Students must do their homework.
A company executive is wise to choose his words carefully.	Company executives are wise to choose their words carefully.
If a manager wants respect, he should behave respectably.	Managers who want respect should behave respectably.

Restructure Sentences to Avoid Gender Reference

Finally, you can avoid gender references altogether by restructuring your sentences. See how this is done in the following examples.

GENDER-SPECIFIC	GENDER-NEUTRAL
Man has always turned to his intellect to solve problems.	People have always turned to their intellect to solve problems.
A company executive is wise to drive himself relentlessly.	Anyone who desires success must work relentlessly.
A nurse must take her job seriously.	A nurse must take the job seriously.
Someone left his umbrella in the cloakroom. He should call Lost and Found.	The person who left an umbrella in the cloakroom should call Lost and Found.
The ladies enjoyed the shopping trip.	The shoppers enjoyed their trip.

Skill Building until Next Time

Pay close attention to the tone and style of everything you write or read. Is the degree of formality appropriate for the message and the audience? Do you sense emotional overload? Is the point of view consistent? Are equivalent ideas presented equally? Does the writing contain gender references? If so, are they likely to offend the reader?

20 ▶ Communicating Your Ideas

LESSON SUMMARY

The previous lessons have dealt with words and sentences. This final lesson is about the bigger issues involved in a piece of writing as a whole. By focusing on the purpose of your writing, you can develop your ideas in a logical, effective way to have the biggest possible impact on your readers.

Mastering writing detail is important, but the main purpose of writing is to communicate a message with a specific purpose to an audience. Most writing does one of three things: inform, explain, or present an argument. Writing effectively involves discovering what you want to say, organizing your ideas, and presenting them in the most logical, effective way. This lesson discusses all of these issues.

▶ Writing to Inform

Good, informational writing is clear, simple, and orderly. In business writing, it's important to get right to the point. No one has time to spend reading your warm-ups, the words you write while you're trying to get to the point. The best communications state the point directly and present the information clearly.

However, sometimes getting started is difficult. Ask yourself a few key questions to help clarify your thoughts and get to the point.

1. Summarize the main idea of your communication in a single sentence. If you can do this, the rest of the writing will come more easily. State it as simply and clearly as possible. If your communication presents a list of information, facts, or statistics, try summarizing the purpose of the information. The sentence should answer the question: Why am I writing this?
2. Next, think about your audience. Who will be reading your writing? What is your relationship with the audience: superior, colleague, customer? Thinking about the audience helps you use an appropriate tone or attitude.
3. Brainstorm all the information that must be included in the communication. This can be in the form of a list or a piece of paper with words and pictures connected by lines; use whatever works best for you. Get all the information down on paper where you can look at it.
4. Once the information is assembled, think about the most efficient way to organize it. Think about your message as a train of thought, one in which all the parts are connected. How can you organize the information in such a way that connections seem easy and natural? Consider these organizational patterns:
   - Spatial order: the order in which items are arranged in relationship to each other
   - Chronological order: time order
   - Logical order: begin with the most basic premise, follow with what can be derived from the premise
   - General to specific: begin with a general statement, arrive at a specific fact
   - Specific to general: arrive at a generalization from a series of specific facts

5. Now it's time to start writing. Begin with a sentence or short paragraph that states the purpose of the communication, revising what you came up with in Step 1 now that you know what your main points are.
6. Develop each of the ideas you identified in Steps 3 and 4 in a single paragraph. If the supporting ideas can be presented as effectively in list form as they can in sentence form, use a bulleted or numbered list similar to this one, which outlines organizational patterns. Stick to one idea in each paragraph and keep the paragraphs as short and concise as possible.

If you're writing for business, use numbered and bulleted lists like the ones on this page. Strive for a clear, logical presentation, one that is well organized and free of excess words that say nothing. Here's a map of one writer's organizational process in responding to a request: the planning, the organization, the main idea, the audience, and the completed memo.

The Planning

Main idea: Ms. Rhinehart has asked for information about our accounting staff (how many, job titles, and levels) and justification for the personnel requests we made.
Purpose: Provide the information so the department can hire additional staff.
Audience: Ms. Rhinehart, vice-president and chief financial officer

I. Data
  A. Current senior staff
    1. One accounting manager
    2. Two senior accountants
    3. Three senior accounts receivable managers
    4. Three senior payroll managers
  B. Current entry-level staff
    1. One assistant to the accounting manager
    2. One assistant to the senior accountants
    3. One assistant to the accounts receivable managers
    4. One assistant to the payroll managers

II. Requests
  A. Additional entry-level staff
    1. Three assistants to provide support to senior accountants, accounts receivable managers, and payroll managers
    2. One assistant to rotate throughout the department as needed
    3. Reason: The acquisition of the new company has doubled the department's workload. At the moment, senior staff members, with high salaries, are spending too much time on entry-level work. Hiring new assistants will allow senior staff to delegate much of this work and return their focus to more complicated projects.
  B. Promoting current staff
    1. Promote assistant to the accounting manager to executive assistant
    2. Reason: In addition to assistant to the accounting manager, the executive assistant can also oversee all department assistants, again relieving the senior staff workload.

The Memo

To: Ms. Rhinehart
From: Allie Leonard
Re: Staff assessment and needs of accounting department as requested
Date: July 7, 2005

I am providing the information you requested about the accounting staff. I am also outlining our requests for hiring additional staff and the reasons for these requests.

This is the staff, both senior and entry-level, that we have at this time.

- One accounting manager and one assistant to the accounting manager
- Two senior accountants and one assistant to the two senior accountants
- Three senior accounts receivable managers and one assistant to the three accounts receivable managers
- Three senior payroll managers and one assistant to the three senior payroll managers

Due to the acquisition of the new company, the accounting department's workload has doubled, and senior staff members are spending too much time performing tasks that can be handled by assistants. We are requesting four more assistants for our department as well as the promotion of one of the existing assistants. One assistant would work with the senior accountant, another would work with the accounts receivable managers, one would assist the payroll managers, and the fourth assistant would rotate as necessary throughout the department. Additionally, we request the promotion of the existing assistant to the accounting manager to executive assistant to the entire department. In this capacity, she will assist the accounting manager as well as oversee all department assistants. These changes will allow the senior staff to focus their time and energy on crucial high-level projects that are currently being ignored.

Thank you for considering our request.

▶ Writing to Explain

Another form of writing you're likely to use often is explanation. You may need to provide reasons for an action or policy, or you may need to explain how a product is used.

For this type of writing, follow the same planning process as you would for a written communication designed to present information.

1. Summarize the main idea and purpose.
2. Determine the audience.
3. Brainstorm ideas.
4. Organize the ideas.
5. Begin by stating the purpose.
6. Develop the ideas in paragraphs.

Keep these tips in mind as you write.

- Present the steps in a logical order. Chronological order is usually best for a process.
- Be certain you've explained each step clearly, accurately, and thoroughly enough so readers can understand.
- Use the facts and examples to support each of your points.
- Pay special attention to the introduction and conclusion. These two paragraphs lay the foundation for understanding and give the reader a quick review of the information you've just presented. Make the beginning and ending paragraphs work for you.

Here's a real-world example: It outlines the planning a writer did before drafting a letter to a customer explaining how to operate a new copy machine.

Main idea: Explain how to use a new copy machine to new customers

Audience: Members of promotional staff at KCBD-TV, all of whom use the copier

Purposes: (1) Clearly explain use, (2) clearly outline maintenance procedures, (3) provide basic troubleshooting suggestions, (4) assure them that the copier is reliable and that service is quick, should they need it.

I. Daily use
  A. Copying
  B. Enlarging/reducing
  C. Handling multiple-page documents
II. Maintenance
  A. Routine
    1. Loading paper
    2. Adding toner
    3. Clearing paper jams
  B. Troubleshooting
    1. Electrical problems
    2. Paper jams
    3. Failure to copy
  C. Calling the technician
    1. Business day number
    2. Emergency service
III. Reliability
  A. Warranties
  B. Weekly maintenance checks
  C. Service
  D. Two-hour replacement guarantee

First paragraph: Everyone in the promotional department at KCBD-TV will find this new Sharp copy machine a huge improvement over the older model. You'll appreciate how easy it is to use this new copier for daily tasks, and anyone can perform the routine maintenance on the machine. This, our most reliable copier, is backed by a long-term warranty and a quick, efficient service plan.

▶ Writing to Persuade

The other most common type of writing involves presenting a clear, convincing argument. Your written communication may be a single message, or it may be the first in a series of exchanges that will eventually result in a compromise. Each type of argument requires a different approach; however, both kinds of persuasive communications must have three common characteristics: logical order, solid support, and credibility.

Logical Order

Even the brightest and best ideas make no impact if a reader cannot recognize or follow them. Arguments must be carefully organized to create the desired effect on the reader.

The strongest positions are the beginning and the ending of a communication. Place your strongest argument in one position or the other and arrange the rest in such a way that they can be clearly stated and easily linked together.

Solid Support

Good persuasion not only makes a clear, strong claim but also proves the claim with solid support. Here are some ways to support your assertions:

- **Examples**, either personal or researched.
- **Objective evidence**, such as facts and statistics.
- **Citing an authority**. Use a qualified, timely authority whose opinions are applicable to your special situations. If the reader is not familiar with the authority, explain why the person is qualified.
- **Analogy**. If you can think of a clear comparison with which the reader is automatically familiar, present the comparison clearly. Carefully point out all the similarities and explain why the comparison is useful and applicable.

If you are supporting a moral or emotional claim, use logic or emotional appeals made with vivid description and concrete language.

Credibility

A written communication is *credible* if the reader believes the writer or finds the writer trustworthy. Regardless of the history between the writer and reader, each communication provides a fresh opportunity to establish credibility.

In any communication, you can establish credibility in one of three ways:

1. **Demonstrate your knowledge of the subject.** Show that you have personal experience that makes your perspective on the subject reliable. If you have no personal experience from which to draw, show that you have consulted a variety of reliable, neutral sources and that your views are based on your research.
2. **Demonstrate fairness and objectivity.** Show that you have taken into account all of the significant viewpoints. Convince your reader that you understand and value other perspectives on the subject and that you see their merit. Show that you have carefully considered all of the evidence, even that which does not support your point of view.
3. **Seek areas of agreement.** This is especially valuable if your communication is the beginning of a process that will result in a compromise. Find out what the viewpoints have in common and begin building trust and credibility on common ground.

Use the same six steps outlined on page 160 to plan a persuasive communication. Examine the following writer's plan for a written communication that argues in favor of a new scheduling policy.

Claim: Store needs a better system for scheduling employees.
Audience: Store's general manager
Purposes: (1) Point out problems inherent in the current policy, (2) outline the qualities a new scheduling policy should have, (3) point out the

advantages of a scheduling policy with those qualities, (4) show that customers will receive better service, (5) show that employees understand and are willing to share the burden of developing and implementing a new policy.

I. Problems with current policy
   A. Based solely upon seniority
   B. Arbitrary within seniority brackets
   C. Equal number for all shifts
      1. Doesn't allow for employees willing to be flexible
      2. Not enough employees during peak sales times
      3. Too many employees during off-peak sales times
      4. Leads to minimal employee commitment
   D. No incentive for good attendance
II. Qualities of an effective scheduling policy
   A. Continues to take seniority into account
   B. Allows for individual preferences
   C. Allows for flex time
   D. Allows for increased numbers during peak times, reduced numbers during off times
   E. Provides an incentive for reliable attendance
   F. Provides an incentive to work least desirable hours

III. Advantages of a policy with these characteristics
   A. Improved customer service
      1. Better service during peak times
      2. Quality service during off-peak times
   B. Less absenteeism
   C. Improved employee morale
   D. Sense of ownership among employees
IV. Development and implementation
   A. Management responsibilities
   B. Employee responsibilities
      1. Committee willing to develop plan during unpaid time
      2. Willing to assume some responsibility for implementation

First paragraph: Since we value customer service, our store needs to develop a scheduling system that will provide better customer service while at the same time fostering an increased sense of commitment among employees.

Whenever you write, keep in mind that you want to present your message as clearly and simply as possible. Write to *express,* not to *impress.* The words should deliver the message, not get in the way of it.

Skill Building until Next Time

Write a memo asking for a raise. If you can do that, you know the time you've spent with this book has been worth your while. Go ahead, do it. Worst case scenario: Whoever reads the memo will speak or write back and deny the request. Even if this happens, your writing will have made an impression. If you presented a few good arguments, they'll stick in your supervisor's mind even if you don't get the raise. The next one will come sooner than it would have if you hadn't written the memo. Best case scenario: You get a raise. How can you lose? Even if you don't send the memo, write it. It will build your confidence, and maybe you'll send it at a more opportune time. You can think about it, revise it, add to it, and then send it.

Whenever you have an idea you want to be taken seriously, write a memo. It won't be long before people begin to notice that you have the power of the pen. A word of caution: Some people are intimidated by others who can write, and they may even try to discourage you. Don't let them. Just use softer words when you write, and write to them often. In time, they will come to appreciate your ideas and your ability.

Posttest

Now that you've spent a good deal of time improving your grammar and writing skills, take this posttest to see how much you've learned. If you took the pretest at the beginning of this book, you have a good way to compare what you knew when you started the book with what you know now.

When you complete this test, grade yourself, and then compare your score with your score on the pretest. If your score now is much greater, congratulations—you've profited noticeably from your hard work. If your score shows little improvement, perhaps you should review certain chapters. Do you notice a pattern to the types of questions you got wrong? Whatever you score on this posttest, keep this book around for review and refer to it when you are unsure of a grammatical rule.

There's an answer sheet you can use for filling in the correct answers on page 165. Or, if you prefer, simply circle the answer numbers in this book. If the book doesn't belong to you, write the numbers 1–50 on a piece of paper and record your answers there. Take as much time as you need to do this short test. When you finish, check your answers against the answer key that follows. Each answer tells you which lesson of this book teaches you about the grammatical rule in that question.

1.	(a)	(b)	(c)	(d)		18.	(a)	(b)	(c)	(d)		35.	(a)	(b)	(c)	(d)
2.	(a)	(b)	(c)	(d)		19.	(a)	(b)	(c)	(d)		36.	(a)	(b)	(c)	(d)
3.	(a)	(b)	(c)	(d)		20.	(a)	(b)	(c)	(d)		37.	(a)	(b)	(c)	(d)
4.	(a)	(b)	(c)	(d)		21.	(a)	(b)	(c)	(d)		38.	(a)	(b)	(c)	(d)
5.	(a)	(b)	(c)	(d)		22.	(a)	(b)	(c)	(d)		39.	(a)	(b)	(c)	(d)
6.	(a)	(b)	(c)	(d)		23.	(a)	(b)	(c)	(d)		40.	(a)	(b)	(c)	(d)
7.	(a)	(b)	(c)	(d)		24.	(a)	(b)	(c)	(d)		41.	(a)	(b)	(c)	(d)
8.	(a)	(b)	(c)	(d)		25.	(a)	(b)	(c)	(d)		42.	(a)	(b)	(c)	(d)
9.	(a)	(b)	(c)	(d)		26.	(a)	(b)	(c)	(d)		43.	(a)	(b)	(c)	(d)
10.	(a)	(b)	(c)	(d)		27.	(a)	(b)	(c)	(d)		44.	(a)	(b)	(c)	(d)
11.	(a)	(b)	(c)	(d)		28.	(a)	(b)	(c)	(d)		45.	(a)	(b)	(c)	(d)
12.	(a)	(b)	(c)	(d)		29.	(a)	(b)	(c)	(d)		46.	(a)	(b)	(c)	(d)
13.	(a)	(b)	(c)	(d)		30.	(a)	(b)	(c)	(d)		47.	(a)	(b)	(c)	(d)
14.	(a)	(b)	(c)	(d)		31.	(a)	(b)	(c)	(d)		48.	(a)	(b)	(c)	(d)
15.	(a)	(b)	(c)	(d)		32.	(a)	(b)	(c)	(d)		49.	(a)	(b)	(c)	(d)
16.	(a)	(b)	(c)	(d)		33.	(a)	(b)	(c)	(d)		50.	(a)	(b)	(c)	(d)
17.	(a)	(b)	(c)	(d)		34.	(a)	(b)	(c)	(d)						

▶ Posttest

1. Which of the following is a sentence fragment (not a complete sentence)?
- **a.** The memo was distributed on Friday.
- **b.** Although the managers and the support staff had been called.
- **c.** The company was being acquired by a large corporation.
- **d.** Be sure to attend the meeting.

2. Which version is correctly capitalized?
- **a.** After we headed west on interstate 70, my uncle Paul informed us that his Ford Taurus was almost out of gas.
- **b.** After we headed west on Interstate 70, my Uncle Paul informed us that his Ford Taurus was almost out of gas.
- **c.** After we headed West on Interstate 70, my Uncle Paul informed us that his Ford Taurus was almost out of gas.
- **d.** After we headed West on interstate 70, my Uncle Paul informed us that his Ford taurus was almost out of gas.

3. Which version is punctuated correctly?
- **a.** That building, with the copper dome is our state capitol.
- **b.** That building with the copper dome, is our state capitol.
- **c.** That building, with the copper dome, is our state capitol.
- **d.** That building with the copper dome is our state capitol.

4. Which version is punctuated correctly?
- **a.** The temperature was eighty degrees at noon; by 6:00 P.M. it had dropped to below forty.
- **b.** The temperature was eighty degrees at noon, by 6:00 P.M. it had dropped to below forty.
- **c.** The temperature was eighty degrees at noon by 6:00 P.M., it had dropped to below forty.
- **d.** The temperature was eighty degrees at noon by 6:00 P.M. it had dropped to below forty.

5. Which version is punctuated correctly?
- **a.** It was one managers' idea to give us a month's vacation.
- **b.** It was one manager's idea to give us a months vacation.
- **c.** It was one manager's idea to give us a month's vacation.
- **d.** It was one managers idea to give us a month's vacation.

6. Which version is punctuated correctly?
- **a.** "Watch out! yelled the police officer. There's an accident ahead."
- **b.** "Watch out!" yelled the police officer. "There's an accident ahead."
- **c.** "Watch out"! yelled the police officer. "There's an accident ahead."
- **d.** "Watch out! yelled the police officer." "There's an accident ahead."

7. Which version used parentheses correctly?
- **a.** We celebrated one wedding anniversary (we'd been married five years at the time), by spending a week in Italy.
- **b.** We celebrated (one wedding anniversary) we'd been married five years at the time, by spending a week in Italy.
- **c.** We celebrated one wedding anniversary we'd been married five years at the time, (by spending a week in Italy).
- **d.** We celebrated one wedding anniversary we'd been married (five years at the time), by spending a week in Italy.

8. Choose the subject that agrees with the verb in the following sentence.

_____ of the musicians have arrived at the concert.

   a. Each
   b. Neither
   c. One
   d. Two

9. Which of the following sentences is most clearly and correctly written?
   a. Bart told us all about the fish he caught while waiting in line at the movie theater.
   b. At the movie theater, Bart told us about the fish he caught while we waited in line.
   c. As we waited in line at the movie theater, Bart told us about the fish he caught.
   d. As we waited in line, Bart told us about the fish he caught at the movie theater.

10. Which version is in the active voice?
   a. The president of the P.T.A. requested donations for the new auditorium.
   b. For the new auditorium, donations had been requested by the P.T.A. president.
   c. Donations for the new auditorium were requested by the president of the P.T.A.
   d. Donations were requested by the P.T.A. president for the new auditorium.

11. Which version has a consistent point of view?
   a. Last Sunday, we went canoeing on the Platte River. You could see bald eagles high in the trees above us.
   b. While we were canoeing last Sunday on the Platte River, high in the trees above us, you could see bald eagles.
   c. We went canoeing last Sunday on the Platte River, and high in the trees above us, we could see bald eagles.
   d. High in the trees above, the bald eagles were looking down at you, as we canoed on the Platte River last Sunday.

12. Which version uses punctuation correctly?
   a. Help! Do you know where I can find a baby-sitter on such short notice.
   b. Help! Do you know where I can find a baby-sitter on such short notice?
   c. Help? Do you know where I can find a baby-sitter on such short notice!
   d. Help: Do you know where I can find a baby-sitter on such short notice?

13. Which of the underlined words in the following sentence should be capitalized?

My <u>brother</u> has been teaching <u>history</u> at the <u>university</u> of California since last <u>fall</u>.

   a. Brother
   b. History
   c. University
   d. Fall

For questions 14 and 15, choose the correct verb form.

14. When she was asked which employee should be promoted, Ms. Garcia _____ Caroline Martin.
   a. has chosen
   b. choosed
   c. choose
   d. chose

15. The snow _____ to fall late yesterday afternoon.
   a. began
   b. begun
   c. had began
   d. begins

16. Which version is most clearly and correctly written?
   a. Jeff told Nathan that his car battery was dead.
   b. When Jeff spoke to Nathan, he said his car battery was dead.
   c. Jeff told Nathan about his dead car battery.
   d. Jeff told Nathan that the battery in Nathan's car was dead.

For questions 17–19, choose the option that correctly completes the sentence.

17. The cat _____ in a patch of sun on the front porch.
   a. is laying
   b. is lying
   c. lays
   d. laid

18. When I heard the unusual sound, I _____ walked through the house and searched each room very _____.
   a. calmly, carefully
   b. calmly, careful
   c. calm, careful
   d. calm, carefully

19. I have _____ idea how these _____ got in my sweater.
   a. know, wholes
   b. know, holes
   c. no, holes
   d. no, wholes

20. Which of the following sentences contains a redundancy? (It repeats words that express the same idea.)
   a. Del shouted as loudly as he could, but no one heard him.
   b. Twenty minutes had passed before the fire trucks arrived.
   c. Yesterday, the senator made the same speech at three different locations.
   d. For a wide variety of different reasons, more people are using computers.

21. Which version has a parallel structure?
   a. He is a man of many talents. He repairs small machines, he cooks gourmet meals, and you should see his lilies and orchids.
   b. He is a man of many talents. There's a talent for repairing small machines, he cooks gourmet meals, and then there are the lilies and orchids.
   c. He is a man of many talents. He repairs small machines, he cooks gourmet meals, and he grows lilies and orchids.
   d. He is a man of many talents: repairing small machines, cooking gourmet meals, and he grows lilies and orchids.

22. Which of the following sentences contains a cliché?
   a. Looking for Harriet's ring was like searching for a needle in a haystack.
   b. The reason I can't have lunch with you is because I have a dentist appointment.
   c. The crooked fence looked like a row of teeth in need of braces.
   d. As costs go up, so do prices.

23. Which version uses periods correctly?
   a. T.J. McCloud and Dr Sheila Brown will represent the U.S. at the 3 PM ceremony.
   b. T.J. McCloud and Dr. Sheila Brown will represent the U.S. at the 3 P.M. ceremony.
   c. T.J. McCloud and Dr. Sheila Brown will represent the US at the 3 P.M. ceremony.
   d. TJ McCloud and Dr Sheila Brown will represent the U.S. at the 3 PM ceremony.

24. Which version is correctly capitalized?
   a. Many Meteorologists are predicting that the West will have the wettest winter on record.
   b. Many meteorologists are predicting that the west will have the wettest winter on record.
   c. Many Meteorologists are predicting that the West will have the wettest Winter on record.
   d. Many meteorologists are predicting that the West will have the wettest winter on record.

25. Three of the following sentences are either run-ons or comma splices. Which one is NOT?
   a. A group of lions is called a pride a group of elephants is called a herd.
   b. Josh told me he would meet us at the zoo at noon, he never showed up.
   c. We waited three hours, finally, Karen decided to give him a call.
   d. A young sheep is known as a lamb, but a young goat is known as a kid.

26. Which version is punctuated correctly?
   a. There are many reasons—aside from the obvious ones—why she is not the right person for this job.
   b. There are many reasons: aside from the obvious ones—why she is not the right person for this job.
   c. There are many reasons—aside from the obvious ones, why she is not the right person for this job.
   d. There are many reasons aside from the obvious ones—why she is not the right person for this job.

27. Which is the correct punctuation for the underlined portion?

The explosion broke several windows in the <u>factory however</u> no one was injured.

   a. factory, however
   b. factory however;
   c. factory; however,
   d. factory, however;

28. Which version uses hyphens correctly?
   a. My soft-spoken brother-in-law did not raise his voice when he saw that his car had been damaged in the parking-lot.
   b. My soft spoken brother-in-law did not raise his voice when he saw that his car had been damaged in the parking-lot.
   c. My soft-spoken brother-in-law did not raise his voice when he saw that his car had been damaged in the parking lot.
   d. My soft-spoken brother in-law did not raise his voice when he saw that his car had been damaged in the parking lot.

29. Which version is punctuated correctly?
   a. Ms. Jeffers who is my physics teacher, coaches the girls' basketball team.
   b. Ms. Jeffers, who is my physics teacher, coaches the girls' basketball team.
   c. Ms. Jeffers who is my physics teacher coaches the girls' basketball team.
   d. Ms. Jeffers who, is my physics teacher, coaches the girls' basketball team.

For questions 30–34, choose the option that correctly completes the sentence.

30. Several manuals, each with detailed instructions, _____ with your new computer.
   a. were sent
   b. was sent
   c. has been sent
   d. sent

31. Jessica and ____ are looking in the grass for one of her earrings; ____ will be hard to find.
   a. me, it
   b. me, they
   c. I, they
   d. I, it

32. Yesterday, I ____ my watch on this table, but now ____ gone.
   a. set, it's
   b. set, its
   c. sat, its
   d. sat, it's

33. I didn't want Lisa's _____ because I knew she would tell me not to _____ the job.
   a. advice, except
   b. advice, accept
   c. advise, accept
   d. advise, except

34. Carlos _____ the basketball team because he had _____ many sports-related injuries.
   a. quite, too
   b. quite, to
   c. quit, to
   d. quit, too

35. Which version is punctuated correctly?
   a. The recreation center will show the following movies: *Charlotte's Web, Jungle Book,* and *Annie,* the cost will be $2.50 per ticket.
   b. The recreation center will show the following movies; *Charlotte's Web, Jungle Book,* and *Annie;* the cost will be $2.50 per ticket.
   c. The recreation center will show the following movies: *Charlotte's Web, Jungle Book,* and *Annie.* The cost will be $2.50 per ticket.
   d. The recreation center will show the following movies—*Charlotte's Web, Jungle Book,* and *Annie.* The cost will be $2.50 per ticket.

36. Which version is punctuated correctly?
   a. Excited about her European vacation Eva spent hours in the bookstore looking at travel guides.
   b. Excited about her European vacation, Eva, spent hours in the bookstore looking at travel guides.
   c. Excited about her European vacation, Eva spent hours in the bookstore looking at travel guides.
   d. Excited about her European vacation Eva spent, hours in the bookstore looking at travel guides.

37. Which version is punctuated correctly?
  a. The woman who lives across the street was born on July 4, 1922, in Washington, D.C.
  b. The woman, who lives across the street, was born on July 4, 1922, in Washington, D.C.
  c. The woman who lives across the street, was born on July 4, 1922 in Washington, D.C.
  d. The woman who lives across the street was born on July 4, 1922 in Washington D.C.

For question 38, choose the correct verb tense.

38. By next fall, I _____ to all fifty of the United States.
  a. would be
  b. should have been
  c. will have been
  d. had been

39. Three of the following sentences are punctuated correctly. Which one is punctuated incorrectly?
  a. My son's baseball game was postponed; it was raining too hard.
  b. Because it was raining too hard; my son's baseball game was postponed.
  c. My son's baseball game was postponed because it was raining too hard.
  d. It was raining too hard, and my son's baseball game was postponed.

40. Which of the following should NOT be hyphenated?
  a. one-fifteen in the morning
  b. the sixteenth-president of the United States
  c. a thirty-second commercial
  d. a thousand-dollar profit

41. In which of the following sentences is the underlined verb NOT in agreement with the subject of the sentence?
  a. There <u>is</u> only one store that sells that brand.
  b. Why <u>are</u> the girls on the team so excited?
  c. Here <u>are</u> the shoes I wanted to show you.
  d. What <u>is</u> the causes of her constant complaints?

42. In which of the following sentences is the underlined pronoun incorrectl?
  a. The teacher who won the award was <u>her</u>.
  b. <u>He and I</u> plan to visit you tomorrow.
  c. When can <u>she</u> come over for dinner?
  d. Both Michael and Steven will finish <u>their</u> homework early.

43. Which version is punctuated correctly?
  a. Dianes' completed forms aren't in our files.
  b. Diane's completed forms are'nt in our files.
  c. Diane's completed forms' aren't in our files.
  d. Diane's completed forms aren't in our files.

44. Which version is written correctly?
  a. <u>Friends'</u> was one of the most popular shows ever on television.
  b. *Friends* was one of the most popular shows ever on television.
  c. "Friends was one of the most popular shows ever on television.
  d. FRIENDS was one of the most popular shows ever on television.

45. Which of the following sentences is in the passive voice?
  a. Every morning this week, Zeke brought bagels to work.
  b. Each day, he selected several different kinds.
  c. Generally, more than half of the bagels were eaten before 9:00.
  d. We've asked him to stop because we've all gained a few pounds.

46. We noticed the _____ of his cologne when he
_____ in front of us.
- **a.** scent, past
- **b.** scent, passed
- **c.** sent, passed
- **d.** sent, past

47. Ian is the _____ of the triplets, but _____ all
the members of his family, he is the only one
with a talent for music.
- **a.** smallest, among
- **b.** smallest, between
- **c.** smaller, between
- **d.** smaller, among

48. _____ the person _____ found my wallet.
- **a.** Your, who
- **b.** Your, which
- **c.** You're, that
- **d.** You're, who

49. I _____ you thought he would be much older
_____ I am.
- **a.** supposed, then
- **b.** suppose, then
- **c.** suppose, than
- **d.** supposed, than

50. Evan doesn't like chocolate; he _____ away his
_____ of cake.
- **a.** through, piece
- **b.** through, peace
- **c.** threw, peace
- **d.** threw, piece

▶ Answer Key

If you miss any of the answers, you can find help for that kind of question in the lesson shown to the right of the answer.

1. b.	Lesson 3	**26.** a.	Lesson 7
2. b.	Lesson 1	**27.** c.	Lesson 6
3. d.	Lesson 4	**28.** c.	Lesson 9
4. a.	Lesson 5	**29.** b.	Lesson 4
5. c.	Lesson 7	**30.** a.	Lesson 12
6. b.	Lesson 8	**31.** d.	Lesson 13
7. a.	Lesson 9	**32.** a.	Lesson 14
8. d.	Lesson 12	**33.** b.	Lesson 17
9. c.	Lesson 15	**34.** d.	Lesson 16
10. a.	Lesson 11	**35.** c.	Lesson 6
11. c.	Lesson 19	**36.** c.	Lesson 4
12. b.	Lesson 2	**37.** a.	Lesson 5
13. c.	Lesson 1	**38.** c.	Lesson 10
14. d.	Lesson 10	**39.** b.	Lesson 6
15. a.	Lesson 10	**40.** b.	Lesson 9
16. d.	Lesson 13	**41.** d.	Lesson 12
17. b.	Lesson 14	**42.** a.	Lesson 13
18. a.	Lesson 15	**43.** d.	Lesson 7
19. c.	Lesson 17	**44.** b.	Lesson 8
20. d.	Lesson 18	**45.** c.	Lesson 11
21. c.	Lesson 19	**46.** b.	Lesson 16
22. a.	Lesson 18	**47.** a.	Lesson 15
23. b.	Lesson 2	**48.** d.	Lesson 14
24. d.	Lesson 1	**49.** c.	Lesson 17
25. d.	Lesson 3	**50.** d.	Lesson 16

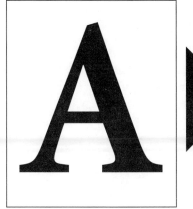

How to Prepare for a Test

 standardized test is nothing to fear. Many people clutch and worry about a testing situation, but you're much better off turning that nervous energy into something positive that will help you do well on your test rather than inhibit your testing ability. The following pages include valuable tips for combating test anxiety—that sinking or blank feeling some people get as they begin a test or encounter a difficult question. Next, you will find valuable tips for using your time wisely and for avoiding errors in a testing situation. Finally, you will find a plan for preparing for the test, a plan for the test day, and a suggestion for a posttest activity.

▶ Combating Test Anxiety

Knowing what to expect and being prepared for it is the best defense against test anxiety, that worrisome feeling that keeps you from doing your best. Practice and preparation keeps you from succumbing to that feeling.

Nevertheless, even the brightest, most well-prepared test takers may suffer from occasional bouts of test anxiety. But don't worry; you can overcome it.

Take the Test One Question at a Time

Focus all your attention on the question you're answering. Block out any thoughts about questions you've already read or concerns about what's coming next. Concentrate your thinking where it will do the most good—on the present question.

Develop a Positive Attitude

Keep reminding yourself that you're prepared. The fact that you have read this book means that you're better prepared than most test takers. Remember, it's only a test, and you're going to do your **best**. That's all anyone can ask of you. If that nagging drill sergeant voice inside your head starts sending negative messages, combat them with positive ones of your own.

- "I'm doing just fine."
- "I've prepared for this test."
- "I know exactly what to do."
- "I know I can get the score I'm shooting for."

You get the idea. Remember to drown out negative messages with positive ones of your own.

If You Lose Your Concentration

Don't worry about it! It's normal. During a long test, it happens to everyone. When your mind is stressed or overexerted, it takes a break whether you want it to or not. It's easy to get your concentration back if you simply acknowledge the fact that you've lost it and take a quick break. You brain needs very little time (seconds really) to rest.

Put your pencil down and close your eyes. Take a few deep breaths and listen to the sound of your breathing. The ten seconds or so that this takes is really all the time your brain needs to relax and refocus .

Try this technique several times in the days before the test when you feel stressed. The more you practice, the better it will work for you on the day of the test.

If You Freeze before or during the Test

Don't worry about a question that stumps you even though you're sure you know the answer. Mark it and go on to the next question. You can come back to the "stumper" later. Try to put it out of your mind completely until you come back to it. Just let your subconscious mind chew on the question while your conscious mind focuses on the other items (one at a time—of course). Chances are, the memory block will be gone by the time you return to the question.

If you freeze before you ever begin the test, here's what to do:

1. Take a little time to look over the test.
2. Read a few of the questions.
3. Decide which are the easiest and start there.
4. Before long, you'll be "in the groove."

▶ Time Strategies

Pace Yourself

The most important time strategy is pacing yourself. Before you begin, take just a few seconds to survey the test, noting the number of questions and the sections that look easier than the rest. Estimate a time schedule based upon the amount of time available to you. Mark the halfway point on your test and make a note beside that mark of what the time will be when the testing period is half over.

Keep Moving

Once you begin the test, keep moving. If you work slowly in an attempt to make fewer mistakes, your mind will become bored and begin to wander. You'll end up making far more mistakes if you're not concentrating.

As long as we're talking about mistakes, don't stop for difficult questions. Skip them and move on. You can come back to them later if you have time. A question that takes five seconds to answer counts as much as one that takes several minutes, so pick up the easy points first. Besides, answering the easier questions first builds your confidence and gets you in the testing groove. Who knows? As you go through the test, you may even stumble across some relevant information to help you answer those tough questions.

Don't Rush

Keep moving, but don't rush. Think of your mind as a seesaw. On one side is your emotional energy. On the other side is your intellectual energy. When your emotional energy is high, your intellectual capacity is low. Remember how difficult it is to reason with someone when you're angry? On the other hand, when your intellectual energy is high, your emotional energy is low. Rushing raises your emotional energy. Remember the last time you were late for work? All that rushing around causes you to forget important things—like your lunch. Move quickly to keep your mind from wandering, but don't rush and get yourself flustered.

Check Yourself

Check yourself at the halfway mark. If you're a little ahead, you know you're on track and may even have some time to check your work. If you're a little behind, you have several choices. You can pick up the pace a little, but do this only if you can do it comfortably. Remember—**don't rush!** You can also skip around in the remaining portion of the test to gain as many easy points as possible. This strategy has one drawback, however. If you are marking a bubble-style answer sheet and you put the right answers in the wrong bubbles—they're wrong. So pay close attention to the question numbers if you decide to do this.

▶ Avoiding Errors

When you take the test, you want to make as few errors as possible in the questions you answer. Here are a few tactics to keep in mind.

Control Yourself

Remember the comparison between your mind and a seesaw that you read about a few paragraphs ago? Keeping your emotional energy low and your intellectual energy high is the best way to avoid mistakes. If you feel stressed or worried, stop for a few seconds. Acknowledge the feeling (Hmmm! I'm feeling a little pressure here!), take a few deep breaths, and send yourself a few positive messages. This relieves your emotional anxiety and boosts your intellectual capacity.

Directions

In many standardized testing situations, a proctor reads the instructions aloud. Be sure you understand what is expected. If you don't, **ask.** Listen carefully for instructions about how to answer the questions and make certain you know how much time you have to complete the task. Write the time on your test if you don't already know how long you have to take the test. If you miss this vital information, **ask for it.** You need it to do well on your test.

Answers

Place your answers in the right blanks or the corresponding ovals on the answer sheet. Right answers in the wrong place earn no points. It's a good idea to check every five to ten questions to make sure you're in the right spot. That way, you won't need much time to correct your answer sheet if you have made an error.

Reading Long Passages

Frequently, standardized tests are designed to test your reading comprehension. The reading sections often contain passages of a paragraph or more. Here are a few tactics for approaching these sections.

This may seem strange, but some questions can be answered without ever reading the passage. If the passage is short, a paragraph around four sentences or so, read the questions first. You may be able to answer them by using your common sense. You can check your answers later after you've actually read the passage. Even if you can't answer any of the questions, you know what to look for in the passage. This focuses your reading and makes it easier to retain important information. Most questions will deal with isolated details in the passage. If you know what to look for ahead of time, it's easier to find the information.

If a reading passage is long and followed by more than ten questions, you may end up spending too much time reading the questions first. Even so, take a few seconds to skim the questions and read a few of the shorter ones. As you read, mark up the passage. If you find a sentence that seems to state the main idea of the passage, underline it. As you read through the rest of the passage, number the main points that support the main idea. Several questions will deal with this information. If it's underlined and numbered, you can locate it easily. Other questions will ask for specific details. **Circle** information that tells who, what, when, or where. The circles will be easy to locate later if you run across a question that asks for specific information. Marking up a passage in this way also heightens your concentration and makes it more likely that you'll remember the information when you answer the questions following the passage.

Choosing the Right Answers

Make sure you understand what the question is asking. If you're not sure of what's being asked, you'll never know whether you've chosen the right answer. So figure out what the question is asking. If the answer isn't readily apparent, look for clues in the answer choices. Notice the similarities and differences in the answer choices. Sometimes, this helps to put the question in a new perspective and makes it easier to answer. If you're still not sure of the answer, use the process of elimination. First, eliminate any answer choices that are obviously wrong. Then, reason your way through the remaining choices. You may be able to use relevant information from other parts of the test. If you can't eliminate any of the answer choices, you might be better off to skip the question and return to it later. If you can't eliminate any answer choices to improve your odds when you come back later, then make a guess and move on.

If You're Penalized for Wrong Answers

You **must know** whether there's a penalty for wrong answers before you begin the test. If you don't, ask the proctor before the test begins. Whether you make a guess or not depends upon the penalty. Some standardized tests are scored in such a way that every wrong answer reduces your score by one-fourth or one-half of a point. Whatever the penalty, if you can eliminate enough choices to make the odds of answering the question better than the penalty for getting it wrong, make a guess.

Let's imagine you are taking a test in which each answer has four choices and you are penalized one-fourth of a point for each wrong answer. If you have no clue and cannot eliminate any of the answer choices, you're better off leaving the question blank because the odds of answering correctly are one in four. This makes the penalty and the odds equal. However, if you can eliminate one of the choices, the odds are now in your favor. You have a one in three chance of answering the question correctly. Fortunately, few tests are scored using such elaborate means, but if your test is one of them, know the penalties and calculate your odds before you take a guess on a question.

If You Finish Early

Use any time you have left at the end of the test or test section to check your work. First, make certain you've put the answers in the right places. As you're doing this, make sure you've answered each question only once. Most standardized tests are scored in such a way that questions with more than one answer are marked wrong. If you've erased an answer, make sure you've done a good job. Check for stray marks on your answer sheet that could distort your score.

After you've checked for these obvious errors, take a second look at the more difficult questions. You've probably heard the folk wisdom about never changing an answer. If you have a good reason for thinking a response is wrong, change it.

▶ The Days before the Test

Physical Activity

Get some exercise in the days preceding the test. You'll send some extra oxygen to your brain and allow your thinking performance to peak on the day you take the test. Moderation is the key here. You don't want to exercise so much that you feel exhausted, but a little physical activity will invigorate your body and brain.

Balanced Diet

Like your body, your brain needs the proper nutrients to function well. Eat plenty of fruits and vegetables in the days before the test. Foods that are high in lecithin, such as fish and beans, are especially good choices. Lecithin is a mineral your brain needs for peak performance. You may even consider a visit to your local pharmacy to buy a bottle of lecithin tablets several weeks before your test.

Rest

Get plenty of sleep the nights before the test. Don't overdo it, though, or you'll make yourself as groggy as if you were overtired. Go to bed at a reasonable time, early enough to get the number of hours you need to function **effectively**. You'll feel relaxed and rested if you've had plenty of sleep in the days before you take the test.

Trial Run

At some point before you take the test, make a trial run to the testing center to see how long it takes. Rushing raises your emotional energy and lowers your intellectual capacity, so you want to allow plenty of time on test day to get to the testing center. Arriving ten or fifteen minutes early gives you time to relax and get situated.

▶ Test Day

It's finally here, the day of the big test. Set your alarm early enough to allow plenty of time. Eat a good breakfast. Avoid anything really high in sugar, such as donuts. A sugar high turns into a sugar low after an hour or so. Cereal and toast, or anything with complex carbohydrates, is a good choice. Eat only moderate amounts. You don't want to take a test feeling stuffed!

Pack a high energy snack to take with you. You may have a break sometime during the test when you can grab a quick snack. Bananas are great. They have a moderate amount of sugar and plenty of brain nutrients, such as potassium. Most proctors won't allow you to eat a snack while you're testing, but a peppermint shouldn't pose a problem. Peppermints are like smelling salts for your brain. If you lose your concentration or suffer from a momentary mental block, a peppermint can get you back on track. Don't forget the earlier advice about relaxing and taking a few deep breaths.

Leave early enough so you have plenty of time to get to the test center. Allow a few minutes for unexpected traffic. When you arrive, locate the restroom and use it. Then find your seat and make sure it's comfortable. If it isn't, tell the proctor and ask to move to something you find more suitable.

Now relax and think positively! Before you know it, the test will be over, and you'll walk away knowing you've done as well as you can.

▶ After the Test

Two things:

1. Plan a little celebration.
2. Go to it.

If you have something to look forward to after the test is over, you may find it easier to prepare well for the test and to keep moving during the test. **Good luck!**

B ▶ Additional Resources

If using this book has whetted your appetite for learning to write better, you may want to continue your study. Many high schools and community colleges offer inexpensive writing courses for adults in their continuing education departments, or you may be able to find a teacher who is willing to tutor you for a modest fee. In addition, you might consult one of the following books:

- *Thirty Days to Better English* by Norman Lewis (Signet)
  Useful for general information; suited to both native and nonnative speakers of English.

- *English Made Simple* by Arthur Waldhorn and Arthur Ziegler (Made Simple Books)
  Designed for nonnative speakers of English; also good for native speakers with little training in grammar.

- *Errors in English and Ways to Correct Them* by Harry Shaw (HarperCollins)
  Addresses specific problems in both writing and grammar; useful for nonnative speakers of English.

- *Grammar* by James R. Hurford (Cambridge University Press)

  Thorough coverage of parts of speech, sentence structure, usage, punctuation, and mechanics; especially good for native speakers of English.

- *Grammar Essentials* by Judith Olson (Learning-Express)

  All the rules of grammar explained in plain English; includes lots of exercises so you can practice what you learn.

- *The Grammar Handbook* by Irwin L. Feigenbaum (Oxford University Press)

  Huge, unfortunately expensive, book; very comprehensive and problem specific.

- *The Handbook of Good English* by Edward D. Johnson (Washington Square Press)

  Well-organized, comprehensive handbook for both grammar and writing.

- *Improve Your Writing for Work* by Elizabeth Chesla (LearningExpress)

  Great instruction on how to write in the business world, as well as tips on good writing in general.

- *Living in English* by Betsy J. Blosser (National Textbook Company)

  Specially designed for nonnative speakers of English.

- *1001 Pitfalls in English Grammar* by Ruth Parle Craig and Vincent F. Hopper (Barron's)

  Problem-solving approach to writing and grammar; very useful for nonnative speakers of English.

- *Practice with Idioms* by Ronald E. Feare (Oxford University Press)

  For nonnative speakers of English.

- *Smart English* by Annette Francis (Signet)

  Thorough general-purpose handbook for both writing and grammar; good for nonnative speakers of English.

- *The New Well-Tempered Sentence: A Punctuation Handbook for the Innocent, the Eager and the Doomed* by Karen Elizabeth Gordon (Houghton Mifflin)

  Interesting general information on punctuation; especially valuable for nonnative and confused native speakers.

- *Writing Smart* by Marcia Lerner (Princeton Review)

  Good for general writing skills; well organized, so information is easy to find.

NOTES

Special FREE Online Practice from LearningExpress!

Let LearningExpress help you acquire essential writing skills FAST

Go to the LearningExpress Practice Center at www.LearningExpressFreeOffer.com, an interactive online resource exclusively for LearningExpress customers.

Now that you've purchased LearningExpress's *Writing Skills Success in 20 Minutes a Day* skill-builder book, you have **FREE** access to:

- **40 questions covering GRAMMAR FOR WRITING** that demonstrate how to choose the correct word for clarity, how to recognize a well written sentence, and how to combine two sentences clearly
- **A FREE Online Essay** to practice your narrative essay writing—**instantly scored**
- **Immediate scoring and detailed answer explanations**
- Benchmark your skills and focus your study with our **customized diagnostic report**

Follow the simple instructions on the scratch card in your copy of *Writing Skills Success*. Use your individualized Access Code found on the scratch card and go to www.LearningExpressFreeOffer.com to sign-in. Start practicing your writing skills online right away!

Once you've logged on, use the spaces below to write in your access code and newly created password for easy reference:

Access Code: _____   Password: _____